YOUR KNOWLEDGE HAS VALUE

Stefan Frisch

Aus der Reihe: e-fellows.net stipendiaten-wissen

e-fellows.net (Hrsg.)

Band 454

The impact of a CEO's task knowledge on the leader life cycles

GRIN Verlag

Bibliografische Information der Deutschen Nationalbibliothek:

Die Deutsche Bibliothek verzeichnet diese Publikation in der Deutschen National-
bibliografie; detaillierte bibliografische Daten sind im Internet über http://dnb.d-
nb.de/ abrufbar.

Imprint:

Copyright © 2011 GRIN Verlag GmbH
Druck und Bindung: Books on Demand GmbH, Norderstedt Germany
ISBN: 978-3-656-22420-4

This book at GRIN:

http://www.grin.com/en/e-book/196180/the-impact-of-a-ceo-s-task-knowledge-on-
the-leader-life-cycles

GRIN - Your knowledge has value

Der GRIN Verlag publiziert seit 1998 wissenschaftliche Arbeiten von Studenten, Hochschullehrern und anderen Akademikern als eBook und gedrucktes Buch. Die Verlagswebsite www.grin.com ist die ideale Plattform zur Veröffentlichung von Hausarbeiten, Abschlussarbeiten, wissenschaftlichen Aufsätzen, Dissertationen und Fachbüchern.

Visit us on the internet:

http://www.grin.com/

http://www.facebook.com/grincom

http://www.twitter.com/grin_com

LEIPZIG GRADUATE SCHOOL OF MANAGEMENT

HHL - Leipzig Graduate School of Management

Chair of Strategic Management and Organization
Master Thesis

The impact of a CEO's
task knowledge on the
leader life cycles

Name, Prename: **Frisch,** Stefan Peter

Leipzig, July 8, 2011

Abstract

Guided by the advancements of research on organizational learning, this thesis theoretically analyzes the impact of different dimensions of a CEO's task knowledge on company performance over the CEO life cycle. For this purpose, it attempts to conceptualize the previously fragmented literatures on company/industry based, experience based and personality based task knowledge into an integrated concept of task knowledge within the leader life cycle theory. As a result of this, consistent hypotheses on the positive influence of higher task knowledge and the concrete impact on the shape of the leader life cycle curve have been derived. Conclusively, the thesis might play a pioneering role within the progression from a pure demographic characteristics based methodology to direct psychological personality measures of an executive's cognitive base. The empirical validation deserves further attention.

Keywords: Leader life cycle theory; CEO life cycle; Task knowledge; Position-specific skills

Table of contents

Table of figures

Table of abbreviations

CEO	Chief Executive Officer
e.g.	for example (latin: exempli gratia)
edn.	edition
eds.	editors
et al.	et alii
etc.	et cetera
i.e.	for example (latin: id est)
ibid.	meaning "the same place" (latin: ibidem)
IT	Information Technology
HR	Human Resources
MBTI	Myers-Briggs-Type-Indicator
NBA	National Basketball Association
p.	page
pp.	pages
TMT	Top Management Team
NBA	National Basketball Association
UK	United Kingdom
US	United States of America

1 Introduction

Almost 20 years ago, Hambrick and Fukutomi revolutionized the CEO-research landscape by explaining a new framework to theorize an inverted curvilinear relationship between a CEO's tenure in office and company performance, the seasons of a CEO's tenure[1]. By doing so, they connected the behavioral CEO features like characteristics or organizational strategies with the temporal dimension of the executive's tenure during his CEO assignment lifecycle. Those few empirical studies, which have tested leader life cycle theory so far, have found general support for the theory's view[2], or at least by allowing for differences in long- or short- tenured leaders[3]. These studies have also shown, however, that the concrete shape of a leader life cycle is dependent on distinct variables. Hambrick and Fukutomi name a small number of factors that determine the exact structure of the life cycle, namely commitment to a paradigm, task knowledge, information diversity, task interest and power[4]. A CEO's task knowledge as one of these factors, forms a crucial behavioral component in determining the exact shape of the leader life cycle and hence the relation to company performance. Strikingly task knowledge variables are broadly researched in upper echelons theory[5] and organizational learning and leadership theories, but not in leader life cycle theory itself. Further, Wulf/ Stubner's[6] prognosticate that an incorporation of position-specific knowledge into executive succession research deserves further attention. Nevertheless, no one has yet examined a more fine grained approach to the impact of a CEO's task knowledge within the leader life cycle. Without this, leader life cycle theory cannot be tested or validated holistically. Thus, it constitutes a necessity to shed light on this factor at the core of the theory, to better understand and to test the underlying mechanism.

(Aim) The aim of this thesis is to transfer strategy-CEO fit research, organizational learning research as well as leadership-based task knowledge research to the leader life cycle theory, and to explore the effect of position-specific skills of a CEO

---

[1] See Hambrick/ Fukutomi (1991).
[2] See Miller/ Shamsie (2001); Giambatista (2004); Henderson/ Miller/ Hambrick (2006).
[3] See Wulf et al. (2010), p. 19.
[4] See Hambrick/ Fukutomi (1991), p. 723.
[5] See Hambrick/ Mason (1984), p. 198.

throughout the seasons of his tenure on company performance. Based on an organizational learning perspective, such a more fine-grained approach needs to analyze the underlying dimensions like organization and industry insiders/ outsiders phrased by Hambrick and Fukutomi[7]. Moreover, it will be essential to add further dimensions having been tested in the fields of organizational learning and upper echelon theories. Not stopping there, the composition of a holistic or integrated task knowledge factor, appropriate to be incorporated into leader life cycle theories, requires specific hypotheses on the impact of company performance. Addressing the question how different dimensions of task knowledge of a CEO influence company performance over his tenure in office, this thesis offers a highly relevant theoretical perspective in the context of the entire CEO life cycle[8]. The derivation of well-founded hypotheses and the determination of an appropriate empirical research setting will close an important research gap concerning the conceptualization of task knowledge in the leader life cycle theory. In short, the **goal** of this thesis is **to theoretically analyze the impact of different dimensions of CEO's task knowledge on company performance over the CEO life cycle.**

(Structure) To achieve these research goals, the thesis is structured as following: First of all, it will be dwelled upon the derivation of typical CEO work roles based on activities to initiate the discussion about what a CEO's tasks are. Further the theoretical foundations of the upper echelons theory contribute to this as a basis for the impact of a CEO on performance. Particularly, the performance during a CEO life cycle is then described by the leader life cycle theory. The depiction of the different seasons of a CEO's tenure as well as the influencing factors, among them task knowledge, will explain the theoretical mechanisms. Additionally it will indicate the limitations of the leader life cycle as a theoretical base for explaining the impact on company performance.

Secondly, chapter three aims to theoretically approach, decipher and conciliate the different notions and facets of task knowledge. To achieve this, a basic

---

[6] See Wulf/ Stubner (2008), p. 32.
[7] See Hambrick/ Fukutomi (1991), p. 725.

understanding of knowledge from a psychological and organizational theoretical perspective will be briefly created to put task knowledge into its original context. Likewise, the motivation theoretical components of task knowledge in leadership theories are counseled, in which skills and knowledge are mostly modeled as traits or contingencies that can foster or indicate motivation or personality[9]. Based on these components characteristics of leader personalities skills useful for CEO jobs can be derived. This shall create an understanding of what task knowledge means, in what concepts it is used and which dimensions of it are relevant for incorporating them into a task knowledge factor of the leader life cycle theory. Hence the question about the origin of task knowledge and its influence on leaders is addressed.

Thereafter chapter four advances to the specific and in the recent scientific discourses not yet discussed topic of the impact of a CEO's task knowledge on the leader life cycle. Therefore a theoretical construct of task knowledge in the leader life cycle will be drawn, which characterizes the influence of a leader's task knowledge during the tenure. Concerning this construct, hypotheses based on the previous theoretical foundations will be constructed to present the impact of a CEO's task knowledge on the company performance in detail. Furthermore this helps to illuminate the connection between CEO task knowledge and the general slope of the leader life cycle.

Chapter five concentrates on preparing the transition of the theoretical construct into an empirical test of the effect of task knowledge on the performance over the CEO life cycle. Hence general remarks are given on how to break down the influencing factors of the concept into variables that can be used in a regression. This will indicate several limitations and implications of the theoretical construct which will be further discussed in is chapter.

Finally, chapter six concludes that task knowledge, as a core factor within the CEO life cycle theory needs to be incorporated into a successful application and test of the theory to its full extent. Hence using the construct and its variables evaluated

---

[8] It partially builds upon Wulf/ Stubner (2008)'s contribution on some aspects of position-specific knowledge in the context of a CEO succession.

[9] See Robbins/ Judge (2009), p. 88 (learning), p. 136 (personality), p. 249 (job characteristics).

in this thesis can be recommended for further empirical and theoretical research on performance during the leader life cycle.

2 Theoretical foundations

2.1. A CEO's tasks and roles

Starting with the endeavor to theorize on a company leader's task knowledge on firm performance during the leader tenure, the role and the respective tasks of a leader or Chief Executive Officer (CEO), has to be defined upfront. At least since Peter Drucker's 1954 book[10], CEOs are described as managers and, in their position at the top of the firms hierarchy, nowadays especially as leaders[11]. Thus as the tasks a CEO performs and his required knowledge matter most for this thesis, no further distinction between managers and leaders is required. CEOs are seen as managers and leaders, or going with Mintzberg "leadership as management practiced well"[12]. Further, to specify what executives really do many researchers studied the nature of executive work and thus believe that the CEO occupies a distinct and unique role due to the nature of the position's personal and organizational characteristics.

Their aim was to identify behavioral roles that characterize managerial work by observing, categorizing, and interpreting chief executive officers at work[13]. Sune Carlson was the first to empirically examine executive behavior in his book in 1951[14]. Moreover, in the early 1970's Henry Mintzberg initiated his research on defining a CEO's job and specified ten management roles corresponding to a CEO's job tasks. Other researchers like John Kotter conducted executive studies starting with his dissertation to explain behavioral patterns of mayors[15] and later to, e.g. add leadership roles[16] or better understand organizations. Likewise in Germany, Reichwald studied executive behavior from an information and

---

[10] See Drucker (1954).
[11] See Mintzberg (2009), p. 1.
[12] See ibid., p. 9.
[13] See Dargie (2000), p. 41.
[14] See Matthaei (2010), pp. 50-51; Carlson (1951).
[15] See ibid., pp. 66-67.
[16] See Kotter (1990), p. 82.

communication technology perspective[17]. Recently Emilio Matthaei analyzed the research area in his doctoral dissertation[18]. And again it was Mintzberg, who reevaluated the job of managers by joining CEOs at work and tried to interpret the tasks and roles that one can derive out of these field experiences[19].

So far, looking at what a CEO really is, the Dictionary of Business Terms denotes him as the "officer who has ultimate management responsibility for an organization" [20]. This means that he e.g. appoints other managing directors of the company and is accountable directly to the company's owners. This short definition explicates already the legal basis for CEO's job which is set up in the respective business laws defining legal forms of companies. He thus is often seen as ultimately responsible and accountable for managing an organization's strategy[21].

Nevertheless, as the aim is to understand what kind of task knowledge managers need or shall have, their job tasks need to be understood more thoroughly. Beyond the legal basis, the mentioned above researchers of the so called Work Activity School mainly draw attention on CEOs job activities and the time distribution of these activities. They finally classify the roles which a CEO plays to fulfill his or her tasks during the activities to define the nature of executive work[22]. Looking at the CEO activities, researchers replaced managerial "folklore"[23] or rhetoric like planning, organizing, coordinating and controlling by facts of what managers do. Mintzberg declares that managers work relentlessly on various brief, fragmented and disconnected, but action-oriented and mostly non routine tasks[24]. Chief executives hereby favor informal communication, like telephone calls, meetings and e-mail, but face increasing complexity through an overload of information spammed by others.[25] This illustrates that managing lateral relationships among colleagues and associates as well as hierarchical

---

[17] See Beckurts/ Reichwald (1984).
[18] See Matthaei (2010), pp. 17-73.
[19] See Mintzberg (2009), p. 17.
[20] Friedman (2007).
[21] See Jaw/ Linb (2009), p. 222.
[22] See Matthaei (2010), pp. 40-8; Mintzberg (2009), p. 48.
[23] Mintzberg (1989).
[24] See Mintzberg (2009), p. 19; See Jaw/ Linb (2009), p. 221.
[25] See Mintzberg (2009), p. 25.

relationships[26] which allows the manager to exercise indirect control[27], is a core task area in management.

The actual tasks that CEOs work on can be clustered and time distribution of the activities can be splitted based on different dimensions like the place of the CEO's work, mode, subject or purpose of the activity or based on details of the contacts[28]. The important results of such an analysis, carried out by Matthaei are that in general most of a CEO's work time is scheduled (60,8%) and most of this is spent on meetings (64,2%). With respect to the subject most of the appointments are related to organizing and planning activities (15,8%). Based on their purpose, activities are predominantly information related such as receiving, reviewing and giving information (35,4%). This is followed by decision making and strategy tasks as well as external board contact, organizational work and ceremonies[29].

Such a dismantling of an executive's activities and time is done by all researchers, for it enables them to *derive work roles.* They can be defined as organized behavioral sets belonging to the CEO position[30]. Researchers have not jet used these roles to construct broader theories of executive behavior[31]; they will be used here – as the most comprehensive available theoretical aggregates – to further deduce the relevant role or task knowledge. As none of them claims to be either complete or mutually exclusive and collectively exhaustive three different categorizations which are surely feasible and appropriate for this purpose will be introduced. They are composed in figure 1. The left list was also the first one and is rather written as task descriptions than concrete roles. They were formulated by Hemphill and e.g. used by Castaldi in 1986[32]. Nevertheless the roles Mintzberg named in his dissertation in 1973 became the most popular ones. However, he revised them in 2009 in his new book on managing, declaring that managerial work is more dimensional than simply putting roles on a list. Finally Matthaei classified a CEO's roles based on his studies of 29 CEOs and did this like

---

[26] See Mintzberg (2009), p. 29; Matthaei (2010), p. 177.
[27] See Mintzberg (2009), p. 32.
[28] See Matthaei (2010), pp. 110-18.
[29] See ibid., pp. 119-20.
[30] See Castaldi (1986), p. 54.
[31] See O'Gorman/ Bourke/ Murray (2005), p. 3.
[32] See Hemphill (1960), p. xiii; Castaldi (1986), p. 54.

Mintzberg in a person/ organization centered way by distinguishing his three main classes of operation, integration and networking roles[33].

Figure 1[34]
CEO roles

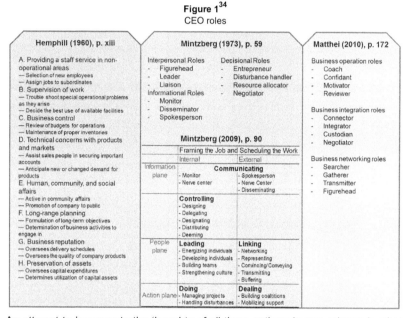

Hemphill (1960), p. xiii	Mintzberg (1973), p. 59		Matthei (2010), p. 172
A. Providing a staff service in non-operational areas	**Interpersonal Roles**	**Decisional Roles**	Business operation roles
— Selection of new employees	- Figurehead	- Entrepreneur	- Coach
— Assign jobs to subordinates	- Leader	- Disturbance handler	- Confidant
B. Supervision of work	- Liaison	- Resource allocator	- Motivator
— Trouble shoot special operational problems as they arise	**Informational Roles**	- Negotiator	- Reviewer
— Decide the best use of available facilities	- Monitor		
C. Business control	- Disseminator		Business integration roles
— Review of budgets for operations	- Spokesperson		- Connector
— Maintenance of proper inventories			- Integrator
D. Technical concerns with products and markets	**Mintzberg (2009), p. 90**		- Custodian
— Assist sales people in securing important accounts			- Negotiator

	Framing the Job and Scheduling the Work		Business networking roles
	Internal	External	- Searcher
Information plane	**Communicating**		- Gatherer
	- Monitor	- Spokesperson	- Transmitter
	- Nerve center	- Nerve Center	- Figurehead
		- Disseminating	
	Controlling		
	- Designing		
	- Delegating		
	- Designating		
	- Distributing		
	- Deeming		
People plane	**Leading**	**Linking**	
	- Energizing individuals	- Networking	
	- Developing individuals	- Representing	
	- Building teams	- Convincing/Conveying	
	- Strengthening culture	- Transmitting	
		- Buffering	
	Doing	**Dealing**	
Action plane	- Managing projects	- Building coalitions	
	- Handling disturbances	- Mobilizing support	

An attempt to incorporate the thoughts of all three authors in one scheme is what figure 2 displays, which is however still mostly oriented on Mintzberg's two-dimensional matrix. Particularly his verbs used to describe the tasks, e.g. communicating, controlling, refer already to the skills that will be needed by a CEO to be successful. Together with Matthaei's differentiation of the broader context of the job figure 2 seems to best incorporate a suitable tasks description to further ask for the relevant CEO knowledge. Emphasizing the "information" within the communication function is taken from Hempill and Matthaeis interpretations. "Future strategizing" stands for an important part of a CEO's actual work on being responsible for the strategic direction of the company.

---

[33] See Matthaei (2010), p. 177.
[34] Own graphic; according to the authors named.

Figure 2[35]
An integrated model of CEO roles

Integrated Work Framing Model		
	Internal	External
Business Networking Roles	**Communicating**	
	- Monitor - Information Nerve Center	- Spokesperson - Information Nerve Center - Disseminating
Business Operation Roles	**Controlling** - Designing - Delegating - Designating - Distributing - Deeming - Asset preserving	
Business Integration Roles	**Leading** - Energizing individuals - Developing individuals - Building teams - Strengthening culture - Connecting/Integrating	**Linking** - Networking - Representing - Convincing/Conveying - Transmitting - Buffering
Strategy Decision Roles	**Doing** - Managing projects - Handling disturbances - Future strategizing	**Dealing** - Building coalitions - Mobilizing support

Moreover, when talking about the nature of managerial work, one has to mention that even if CEOs are generally involved in the same type of activities, they will vary across job contexts, companies and industries. E.g. someone managing a consulting firm spends significant time on selling, likewise the chief executive at Boeing also needs to be a good sales person even though the job contexts are quite different[36]. For instance in manufacturing companies products are sold in little bits and pieces, so the chief executive job would not to sell products, but to facilitate venturing[37]. Even though the roles mentioned above describe

---

[35] Own composition.
[36] See Kesner/ Sebora (1994), p. 335.
[37] See McCarthy (2000), p. 38.

idiosyncratic elements of a CEO's job, it is difficult to identify systematic activities that cover all CEOs' jobs[38]. Phrased differently, leaders will set their priorities and leadership styles also based on the environment. Conclusively this kind of environment-based task knowledge will be evaluated separately, because even Mintzberg himself has stated that research on managerial tasks and roles has yet failed to build a comprehensive model of managerial work.[39] Likewise Hales in his 1986 review of some CEO observation studies highlighted the lack of theory development in this research area.

However, as tasks and managerial roles affect the directions of managers' behavior based on their characteristics[40], they can be used to draw the mechanisms of how managers influence company performance. More specifically this is also the starting point of how managers can outperform other managers over their lifecycle when being assigned roles that obtain their specific task knowlege. Those who have performed jobs and acquired the knowledge about certain roles will have an advantage in the future.

2.2. Upper echelon theory

Following the introduction of the CEO's role and tasks, it might be asked why these investigations are important in a business context. As business performance is the result of sound overall company operations, it has long been discussed which influence a CEO would have – if at all – on such a defining success variable[41]. In 1984 Mason and Hambrick initially studied upper echelons to enquire "why organizations act as they do"[42] finding that strategic decision makers can ultimately exert influence on strategy directions and hence company performance. Upper Echelon Theory argues that "organizational outcomes-both strategies and effectiveness are viewed as reflections of the values and cognitive bases of

---

[38] See Jaw/ Linb (2009), p. 221.
[39] See Mintzberg (1994); O'Gorman/ Bourke/ Murray (2005), p. 3/7.
[40] See Hackman (1969), p. 436.
[41] See Mackey (2008), p. 1357.
[42] Hambrick/ Mason (1984), p. 193.

powerful actors in the organization"[43].Towards this, three fundamental thoughts in their paper were that[44]

    a. if one wants to understand why organizations do what they do, and why they perform in their way, one needs to understand the experiences, values, motives, and biases of the top executives;

    b. the top-management team characteristics matter a lot to interpret organizational outcomes – it is not just the CEO;

    c. intangible psychological properties and dispositions can be described by demographic characteristics e.g. tenure, functional background, and education can be used as partial indicators or proxies.

These arguments shall be elaborated further as especially c) is a strong reference point in the further CEO life cycle theory. Since then it was researched intensively, whether and to what extent a positive relationship of a CEO on a company performance could be identified[45].

Historically the 1984 paper brought back chief executive managers or upper echelons into the theoretical frameworks of management scientists, which was before that largely shaped by the so called population ecologists' view which assumed that organizations are bound by inertia and swept along by external forces leaving little influence for top management[46]. This seemed to be short sighted as the CEO usually is the organization's most powerful actor and leader[47]. Hence Hambrick and Mason broke with this view of treating organizations as "quasi individuals"[48] and created a theoretical framework that combines previous works from different research disciplines with regard to upper echelon characteristics[49].

As such, the theory is built on the premise of bounded rationality of the most powerful actors believing that behavioral factors and idiosyncrasies of decision makers will influence results more than finding the right microeconomic

---

[43] Hambrick/ Mason (1984), p. 193; See Kauer (2008), p. 17; Manner (2010), p. 55.
[44] See for this and the following Cannella (2001), pp. 37-8; Nishii/ Gotte/ Raver (2007), p. 3.
[45] See Michl et al. (2010), p. 85.
[46] See Cannella (2001), p. 37.
[47] See Wu/ Levitas/ Priem (2005), p. 859.
[48] See Kauer (2008), p. 17.
[49] See Manner (2010), p. 55.

optimization mechanism[50]. Thus each decision maker brings his cognitive base to an administrative situation, which consists of "knowledge or assumptions about future events, knowledge of alternatives, and knowledge of consequences attached to alternatives"[51]. Figure 3 represents this scheme, highlighting the locus of this kind of task knowledge.

Figure 3[52]
Strategic choice under conditions of bounded rationality

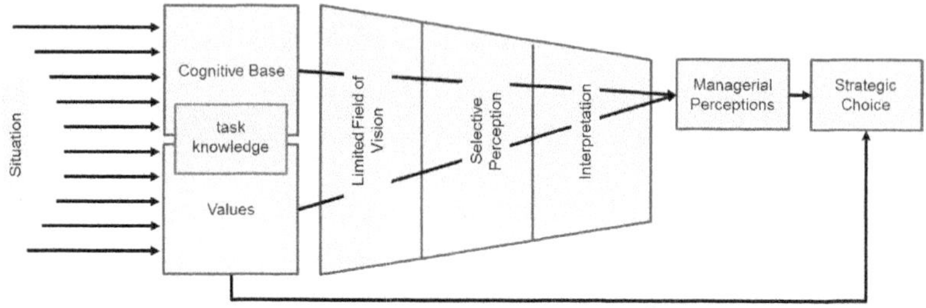

The values and cognitive basis of a CEO are powerful factors influencing the organization. In this thesis it is added that both are largely shaped by the task knowledge as indicated by the red shaped box. Phrasing it differently the upper echelon characteristics will to a large extent also contain dimensions of task related knowledge. Mason and Hambrick explain that depending on an executive's cognitive base and his values[53], which are expressed by the so-called upper echelons characteristics, he will have a restricted field of vision and only selectively perceives the situation he is exposed to. The individual interpretation of the situation, filtered by the background characteristics, leads to his own managerial perception that will be the basis for his strategic decision[54]. As the arrows indicate, his cognitive base and values will have both, a direct and a mediated effect on company performance. The model hence tries to explain the

---

[50] See Hambrick/ Mason (1984), p. 194.
[51] Hambrick/ Mason (1984), p. 195.
[52] See Hambrick/ Mason (1984), p. 195; – red box added. Task knowledge is placed between the cognitive base and the values, as beliefs and assumptions about the future are often value driven.
[53] And here specifically his task knowledge is meant.
[54] See Manner (2010), p. 55.

unique biases and dispositions of top executives under uncertainty and link them as relevant to organizational performance[55].

Figure 4[56]
An upper echelons perspective of organizations

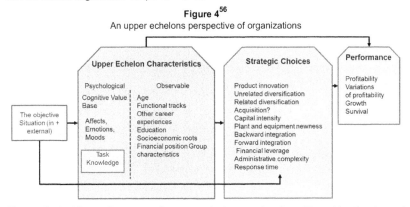

Figure 4 elucidates the *general upper echelon mechanism*. The objective in and external situation of the organization is interpreted by the upper echelon based on his psychological and observable characteristics. They influence performance directly and indirectly; indirectly due to the strategic choices that also are shaped by the characteristics. The specifications in the boxes of Figure 4 hence lay out the research design naming observable indicators which can be used as variables to empirically test the theory – which has been done comprehensively to date. 23 years later, in his 2007 update of upper echelon theory, Hambrick notes that researchers have found substantial evidence to support the relationship between many characteristics and strategic decisions and firm performance outcomes[57]. An earlier review from 2004 concludes that the validity of the upper echelon model has shown to hold within various business settings, strategic choice options and performance metrics[58].

Part of the success of Upper echelon theory was the approach to test the association between the observable characteristics of top executives – which to a large extend are influencing a CEO's task knowledge, as will be shown later –and

[55] See Kauer (2008), p. 17; See Hambrick (2007), p. 334.
[56] See Hambrick/ Mason (1984), p. 198; gray box added by Michl et al. (2010), p. 86; – red box added.
[57] See p. 335; See Manner (2010), p. 56; Patzelt/ zu Knyphausen-Aufseß/ Nikolw (2008), p. 205.
[58] See Carpenter/ Geletkanycz/ Sanders (2004), p. 774.

organizational characteristics[59]. It has to be acknowledged specifically that Hambrick and Mason propose these variables to empiricalize and thus explain complex psychological and cognitive processes[60]. Nevertheless critics argue that due to the individual differences in the cognition of CEOs individual beliefs should be rather measured directly, not proxied by demographics characteristics as substitutes which are seen as too "rough surrogates"[61].

Conclusively, mainly due to the impracticability of direct belief measures[62], many researchers followed the approach of indicating psychological beliefs by observable characteristics. Variables like tenure, education level, and functional background, have shown to represent valid proxies for their cognitions, skills, and values as they powerfully explain for variations in their strategic choices[63]. The reasoning behind age or tenure was that youthful managers were associated with corporate growth[64]. Functional track is generally assumed to proxy the experience someone brings in from his primary functional area. Other career experiences would likewise have a significant effect on the types of actions a CEO takes. Formal education yields to some degree the breadth of an executive's knowledge and skill base. Socioeconomic backgrounds are often used as distinguishing characteristics in demographic studies and hence those of senior executives are also assumed to affect their actions. Finally the effect of a CEO's financial position i.e. due to stock ownership as well as the effect of top management team composition[65] on company performance has been studied at length by researchers in the field.

In a second stage of upper echelon research many scholars tried to explain belief based theoretical constructs by the proposed upper echelon characteristics and then draw based on these constructs conclusions about the changes in

---

[59] See Manner (2010), p. 56.
[60] This thesis follows this approach to theoreize on task knowledge.
[61] Markoczy (1997), p. 1239. Markoczy however also claims in her 2004 paper on cooperation that grand and broad theories with little predictive power and less empirically proveable mechanisms have an intrinsic value as they add „understanding" – leaving open how this may be veryfied. Nevertheless the model proposed by Markoczy and Goldberg 1995 is worth to be considered.
[62] See Hambrick (2007), p. 337.
[63] See Manner (2010), p. 55; Jaw/ Linb (2009), p. 222; Nishii/ Gotte/ Raver (2007), p. 3; Hambrick (2007), p. 335.
[64] See for this and the following Hambrick/ Mason (1984), pp. 198-202.
[65] As the sole focus is the CEO, only little to no attention will be paid to these "out of scope" factors.

organizational outcomes[66]. During this process mediating and moderating variables like how much managerial discretion exists or what an executive's job demands, draw straightforward implications for upper echelons theory[67]. Likewise, Finkelstein's methodology for measuring executive power was comprehensive and well validated[68]. Other research streams analyzed the effect of given incentives, team integration, and team processes as moderating variables[69]. Figure 5 merges some of these insights by presenting a modern path model of upper echelons theory.

[handwritten: Combining through testable & quantifiable construct.]

Figure 5[70]
Path model of modern upper echelon theory

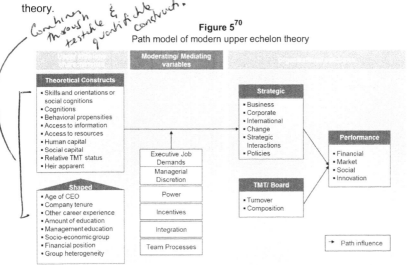

As figure 5 indicates researchers moved to more relevant and hence more complex theoretical or psychological constructs which can be proxied by upper echelon characteristics[71]. Additionally the impact of the moderating and mediating variables had to be considered when drawing conclusions on the influence of the

[66] See Carpenter/ Geletkanycz/ Sanders (2004), p. 759; or exemplary Nishii/ Gotte/ Raver (2007), p. 12; Seaton/ Boyd (2010), p. 74; Jaw/ Linb (2009), p. 229; Reutzel/ Belsito (2010), pp. 11-12.
[67] See Hambrick/ Finkelstein (1987), pp. 378-379; Hambrick/ Finkelstein/ Mooney (2005), p. 472; Hambrick (2007), p. 335; Chaganti/ Sambharya (1987), p. 394.
[68] See Hambrick (2007), p. 335.
[69] See Carpenter/ Geletkanycz/ Sanders (2004), p. 760.
[70] Figure 5 is based on insights from Hambrick (2007) merged with the model proposed by Carpenter/ Geletkanycz/ Sanders (2004, p. 760) ; It however leaves out the antecedents which are not important in a path model. The interested reader is kindly refered to Carpenter/ Geletkanycz/ Sanders (2004), pp. 762-7.
[71] See Michl et al. (2010), p. 80.

psychological constructs on organizational outcomes. Nonetheless, the basic finding, that

> *(1) executives act on the basis of their personalized interpretations of the strategic situations they face, and (2) these personalized construals are a function of the executives' experiences, values, and personalities.*[72]

is still valid[73].

To further open the black box of the executive's personality enables researchers to generate insights on how to surmount or overcome the biases associated with their experiences and dispositions[74]. An important and intensely discussed application example of the theory was research conducted on senior executive tenure. On the one hand, e.g. long-tenured CEOs were shown to increase the probability of successful acquisitions[75], on the other, increasing tenure makes executives less adaptive to change[76]. Researchers willing to find out why tenure matters came up with the idea that initially deeper relevant knowledge of internal processes or established relationships might positively affect company outcomes[77]. Exactly this research stream and disccussion connects upper echelon theory with the leader life cycle theory – or more correctly, at this point leader life cycle theory was born out of upper echelon theory.

2.3. Leader life cycle theory

In order to explore the actual changes in information processing behaviors of managers over their tenure and thereby achieve both, improving upper echelons theory and gaining practical insights for CEOs, Hambrick and Fukutomi formulated the leader life cycle theory by composing "the seasons of a CEO's tenure"[78]. To explain the different interpretations of tenure, they referred to Eitzen and Yetman,

---

[72] Hambrick (2007), p. 334.
[73] See Mackey (2008), p. 1364.
[74] See Hambrick (2007), p. 337.
[75] See Bergh (2001), p. 603; Carpenter/ Geletkanycz/ Sanders (2004), p. 763.
[76] See Miller (1991), p. 49; Hambrick (2007), p. 337.
[77] See Carpenter/ Geletkanycz/ Sanders (2004), p. 763.
[78] Hambrick/ Fukutomi (1991), p. 719.

who had studied a significantly large sample of college basketball coaches to acknowledge an average performance peak after 13 years of office[79],

Their theory, on which this thesis primarily builds, predicts an inverted curvilinear relationship between a CEO's tenure in office and company performance[80]. The curvilinearity is explained by the 5 seasons which are depicted in Figure 6. Hambrick and Fukutomi theorize that when entering a new job, a CEO will dedicate his attention and actions to fulfilling the mandate. It is implicitly associated to his position – the expectations can vary between extreme change and continuity. Willing to create something new, the CEO is likely to start a period of open-mindedness and experimentation after achieving some early successes and gaining a political foothold due to a positive going-in mandate phase[81].

Figure 6[82]
CEO life cycle for stable industries

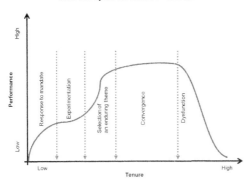

Reflecting often subconsciously on everything he or she has tried during the first two stages of the tenure, the executive selects a theme assembled of features that he believes can successfully and comfortably constitute how the organization should be run from that point on[83]. Having chosen the theme, the CEO begins to reinforce and strengthen it through a sequence of relatively incremental actions supporting and converging on it. Finally the peak will be reached. During longer

[79] See Eitzen/ Yetman (1972), p. 115.
[80] See for this and the following Hambrick/ Fukutomi (1991), p. 727.
[81] See ibid., p. 728.
[82] Figure 6 is drawn according to leader life cycle theory as proposed in Hambrick/Fukutomi (1991).
[83] See for this and the following Hambrick/ Fukutomi (1991), pp. 730-31.

incumbency, negative habituation will overshadow the gains especially the increasing task knowledge – from an organizational perspective: the executives become dysfunctional.

Logically one would ask on which fundamentals this life cycle theory is based and how the different phases can be distinguished. On the former, Hambrick and Fukutomi dedicate two elements, the CEO's paradigm and his entry conditions. As a CEO's job is highly complex and multifarious, no one can comprehend all stimuli and bounded rationality is assumed. This means that the CEO operates with a paradigm – "a finite model ... of how the environment behaves, what options are available, and how the organization should be run"[84].

The paradigm comprises of two components, the schema and the repertoire of the CEO. A schema, derived from cognitive sciences[85], can be seen as the system of preexisting knowledge or personal givens, the "conscious and unconscious preconceptions, beliefs, inferences, and expectations" of a manager[86]. Hence his decision making is based on his schema, which can be traced back from his personal and interpersonal experiences, networks and observations. Secondly an executive's paradigm is formed by the repertoire, his "supply of skills, devices, or expedients"[87], or in other words, his "partly full tool kit"[88].

Finally the entry conditions into the CEO position, such as the prevailing company performance conditions and expectations, together with the mandate, the CEO characteristics, his paradigm and the initial actions will shape the tenure[89].

Prior research and theory have indicated, however, that the concrete shape of a leader life cycle is dependent on distinct moderating variables. To hence answer the latter question on how the different phases can be distinguished, Hambrick and Fukutomi name five "Critical Trends" or factors – commitment to paradigm, task knowledge, information diversity, task interest, and power – that determine the exact structure of the life cycle. Figure 8 graphs the evolution of these dimensions over the CEO's tenure. The proposed distinct phases of a CEO

---

[84] See Hambrick/ Fukutomi (1991), p. 721.
[85] E.g. see Davis (1991), p. 21; or Anderson (1977), pp. 418-19.
[86] See for this and the following Hambrick/ Fukutomi (1991), p. 721.
[87] Merriam-Webster Dictionary (2011a).
[88] Hambrick/ Fukutomi (1991), p. 721.

become visible through their interaction. Avertedly, every season is linked to specific executive behavior and performance, based on the individual shape of the critical trends.

Figure 7[90]
The critical factors within the five seasons of a CEO's tenure

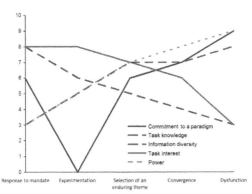

As the figure indicates, the theory postulates that the CEO tenure is determined by the plotted changes[91]. Thus the initial actions of the CEO will be shaped by a moderate commitment to his paradigm, low, but rapidly increasing task knowledge and power, unfiltered sources of information, and a high interest in his task. During the experimentation stage the CEO experiments to find a new paradigm or manifest the old one, hence his commitment could also be strong in some cases. Once he has selected his enduring theme, the commitment to it increases from there on. The task knowledge can also increase slightly. His information sources will be more and more filtered to fit the paradigm and the task interest is declining, as he works on creating a comfortable routine. Nevertheless, the power increases strongly. Finally at the end stage where a CEO becomes dysfunctional, his commitment to paradigm, his power as well as his task knowledge have peak. However, the trend he follows is no longer the best strategy for the company, as

---

[89] See ibid., p. 722.
[90] See Davies/ Thomas (2009), p. 1403; According to Hambrick/ Fukutomi (1991), p. 729. (See Appendix 1) text translated to a 0-10 scale.
[91] See for this and the following Hambrick/ Fukutomi (1991), pp. 727-32.

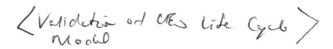

he becomes more and more isolated due to filtered information and shows little interest in his routine-like task.

Hitherto, starting in 2000, only few empirical studies that have tested leader life cycle theory, but all of them have found general support for the theory.

The first study, executed by Miller and Shamsie in **2001** examined major **Hollywood film studios heads** from 1936 to 1965[92]. They confirmed an inverse U-shaped relationship between top executive tenure and an organization's financial performance. Further they observed product line experimentation to deteriorate with increasing executive tenures and to be more likely to positively influence financial performance if the CEO is more experienced. These findings comprise a three-stage 'executive life cycle' which starts with experimentation to learn about their business; to use their accumulated knowledge to increase performance and finally reduce experimentation with performance declining, which occurred quite lately – after 15 years in office.

With "Jumping through hoops", in **2004** and again in the US, Giambatista analyzed of **basketball coaches from the NBA** starting at the league's inception in 1946 until season 2001/2002 in the light of leader life cycle theory[93]. This article encountered support for leader life cycle theory among NBA coaches; generally positive linear and negative quadratic terms were significant. Based on their other hypotheses they could furthermore confirm a life cycle containing seasons of initial disruption, learning based performance gains over the first 3 years and some degree of later stagnation.

Next, in **2005**, the first business application followed as Wu, Levitas, and Priem draw a sample of 84 united States–based, **publicly traded biotechnology companies** active in research during 1992–96[94]. Again, the authors can verify their general hypotheses that the CEO life cycle follows a curvilinear, inverted u-shaped overall relationship between CEO tenure and invention. Moreover, as they inspect how technological dynamism moderates the relationship, they detect that it shifts the curve as short-tenured CEOs will produce more invention within dynamic

---

[92] See for this and the following Miller/ Shamsie (2001), pp. 725, 739.
[93] See for this and the following Giambatista (2004), pp. 614, 617, 619.
[94] See for this and the following Wu/ Levitas/ Priem (2005), pp. 859, 863.

environments, whereas long-tenured CEOs will engage in invention under more stable technological conditions.

Asking how quickly CEOs do become obsolete, Henderson, Miller and Hambrick brought up a similar argument to claim that industry dynamism is an important exogenous factor for leader life cycle theory[95]. In **2006** they asses 326 CEO tenures of **computer and food industry** companies between 1955 and 1994. Consistent with their initial hypothesis they can validate an inverted u-shaped relationship between tenure and profitability in each of their specifications. Furthermore, in contrast to prior research which generalizes adaptive learning advantages[96], they only found performance improvements to be contingent to a stable external environment[97]. In the fast-paced computer industry time related performance improvements were not possible and the performance over the CEO tenure declined steadily. Hence in dynamic environments, due to relatively fixed paradigms and organizational inertia, the experimentation phase of a leader lifecycle would not enhance performance. In line with previous theory firm-level performance dropped only after 10–15 years of CEO tenure within the food industry.

Another study from **2009** by Davis and Thomas surveys **business school deans in the UK** applies the *methodology* of leader life cycle theory[98]. Even though the study is based on 16 semi-structured interviews Myers-Briggs Type Indicator (MBTI) questionnaires completed by the deans the authors use the executive life cycle as a theoretical framework to understand the dean's role. They introduce the executive life cycle model to discover indicative support for the theory, which they e.g. find by describing that a phase of response to mandate as well as experiencing a lapse into weaker performance or dysfunction.

---

[95] See for this and the following Henderson/ Miller/ Hambrick (2006), pp. 447, 451, 458.
[96] See Miller, (1991), p. 35; Miller and Shamsie (2001), p. 738.
[97] This is however not too controversial, as Miller/ Shamsie (2001, p. 739) already note that In stable industries, the learning phase may be quite short and uneventful, while the harvest phase might be long. In uncertain and competitive environments the learning phase may be lengthy and the harvest phase much shorter.
[98] See for this and the following Davies/ Thomas (2009), pp. 1396, 1402, 1406.

Finally Manner **2010** studies a sample of **650 US CEOs and public firms** in order to specify the impact of CEO characteristics on Corporate Social Performance[99]. He refers to leader life cycle theory in his robustness analysis, where he reasons on the basis of tentative evidence that the CEOs' personalities were influencing strategy related variables over time. Similarly he argues that the lack of significant incremental predictive power of the CEO characteristics beyond his medium tenure group might be related to the fact that a CEO has chosen his enduring scheme and will make fewer changes from there on.

3 A theory of task knowledge

3.1. From organizational to individual knowledge

So far, the characteristics of CEO tasks and roles as well as Hambrick and Mason's idea that organizational outcomes can be viewed as reflections of the values and cognitive bases of CEOs based on their characteristics have been constituted. Both have revealed themselves as being essential foundations of the leader life cycle theory. They constitute the relevant preconditions in indicating where task knowledge as a construct is placed within these theories and for which tasks of a CEO knowledge is required or useful. It also clarified, where task knowledge as a critical trend is placed within the leader life cycle theory. Hence now task knowledge as a psychological construct of a CEO's personality can be filled with the relevant dimensions of its meaning and as such it can be reintegrated into the leader life cycle theory to enhance the explanatory power.

Starting generically, the Merriam-Webster Dictionary defines knowledge as "the sum of what is known [or] the body of truth, information, and principles"[100]. As such, knowledge can be seen on both levels, as general – or in this case organizational – knowledge and as individual knowledge – referring to the specific knowledge of the CEO.

---

[99] See for this and the following Manner (2010), pp. 53, 58, 62.
[100] Merriam-Webster Dictionary (2011b).

Within the **organizational context**, Peter Drucker emphasized the words "knowledge society" and "knowledge worker"[101], claiming that knowledge is the only meaningful resource which companies can use in today's dynamic and globalized world to generate competitive advantages in order to stipulate the organizational outcomes[102]. The ability to create organizational knowledge implies that a company can use its capability to create new knowledge and innovate continuously[103]. Organizational knowledge is seen as the firm's capacity to differentiate itself from competition[104]. Subsequently researchers clearly link knowledge to positively affect company performance[105]. Therefore, they sometimes even referred to it as a "knowledge assets"[106]. Even from this organization psychological research stream knowledge is seen as something that deserves attention as it affects company performance.

The **individual knowledge** becomes involved as knowledge sharing to leverage the organizational capabilities has become a core challenge to optimally use the knowledge assets[107]. In the best case, an organization should not only be flat and empowering, but also encompass perpetual learning to form knowledge workers[108]. Organizations distinguish between codified knowledge e.g. as documents, and uncodified or personal knowledge i.e. as information and advice from colleagues[109]. Thus activating and sharing codified and uncodified knowledge as a core competency has become a key success factor in modern organizations. Hence knowledge- and skill-centric organizations had to move from secretly protecting core competencies to efficiently and effectively managing knowledge[110]. *Managing knowledge* mostly contains assigning tasks, enabling knowledge acquisition through training, and sustaining the knowledge within the organization at all levels of the hierarchy[111]. Interestingly, again researchers investigate the

---

[101] Drucker, (1993), p. 6.
[102] See Nonaka/ Takeuchi (1995), p. 3; Haas/ Hansen (2002), p. 1, Drucker, (1993), p. 6.
[103] See Nonaka/ Takeuchi (1995), p. 3.
[104] See King/ Zeithaml (2003), p. 764.
[105] See Haas/ Hansen (2002), p. 1; von Krogh/ Nonaka/ Rechsteiner (2011), p. 1.
[106] Haas/ Hansen (2002), p. 1.
[107] See Chen/ Hwang/ Raghu (2010), p. 22.
[108] See Stuart (1999), p. 39.
[109] See Haas/ Hansen (2002), p. 2.
[110] See Stuart (1999), p. 47.
[111] See Chen/Edgington (2005), p. 309.

impact, this time of knowledge management on company performance and report positive results[112].

As such organizational knowledge which fructifies itself within the organization always depends on the social context, and it is arguable in how far it can be traced back to individuals[113]. Nevertheless, looking at concepts on how to measure organizational knowledge, interviewing CEOs at some point is quite popular, because they play a vital role in managing this resource[114]. Effective leaders can actively destroy knowledge inertia, initiate knowledge transfer programmes and continuous learning, or introduce knowledge IT and HR based knowledge management strategies[115]. This means that the **individual personality and skills** of a leader can and do guide the organizational knowledge.

Consequently Gourlay denotes that knowledge is often redefined within an organizational context into leaders' beliefs as they access the viability and validity of information and ideas[116]. Hence it is the leaders who decide about what kind of knowledge is valuable for the organization. They are governed by their beliefs and criteria such as budget constraints, product life cycles and technological trends which does by no means compare to the philosophical definition of knowledge as it should be based on objective, scientific criteria of verification[117]. Hence the CEO can play an active role in defining the organizational outcome by (a) indirectly filtering organizational knowledge, (b) forming and leveraging his own experience based knowledge, and (c) bringing in his personality and interpersonal skills as Figure 8 indicates.

---

[112] See Chen/ Hwang/ Raghu (2010), p. 22; Andone (2009), p. 25.
[113] See King/ Zeithaml (2003), p. 764.
[114] See ibid., p. 766.
[115] See Lakshman (2005), p. 430.
[116] See Gourlay (2006), p. 1416.
[117] See von Krogh/ Nonaka/ Rechsteiner (2011), p. 12.

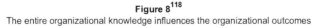

Figure 8[118]

The entire organizational knowledge influences the organizational outcomes

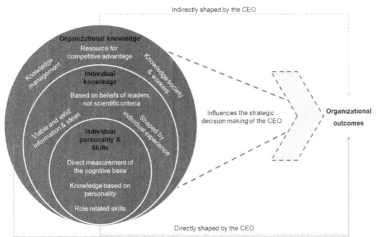

Thus from the organizational perspective knowledge is highly shaped by the leaders and their beliefs on how the organization should develop and which knowledge resources are valuable. In other words, organizational knowledge is largely shaped by the individual knowledge base of the CEO. Again, this is not quite different from just reversely phrasing Mason and Hambrick's upper echelon theory. Nevertheless, it indicates the significance of the need to study the top executive's cognitive base and his individual believes, because they will shape how he understands and carries out his day to day work. By following exactly this direction, organization theorists and cognitive psychologists would go beyond Mason and Hambrick and like e.g. Markoczy claims that capturing individual CEO characteristics is not satisfactory for describing his relevant cognitive base[119].

For the individual CEO beliefs he likewise claims that they do not necessarily need to be knowledge in the sense of scientific justification to affect decisions. With regard to the individual knowledge, whether it affects decisions should be the necessary condition rather than its objective truth. Figure 8 shows that this is also the relevant link between the leader and the organizational outcome and hence

---

[118] Own graphic.
[119] See for this and the following Markoczy (1997), p. 1230.

theory should focus on this one. It will be sufficient if the CEO judges some concepts or relationships to be true beliefs, therefore – on the individual assessment level – those personal perceptions have to be added to knowledge in order comprise the executives individual cognition. On the level of organizational knowledge, researchers investigate even knowledge life cycles[120]. For the individual perspective one needs to note that knowledge and skills as intangibles are non-static and can be cultivated by training or deteriorated though obsolescence[121].

3.2. Psychological dimensions of personality and individual task knowledge

It is now essential to further explore the psychological concepts used to measure the skill set and knowledge base of leaders. They lay the foundations for a CEO's task knowledge or his relevant cognitive base which he needs to accomplish his tasks. The individual cognitive base is, as just developed, largely shaped by CEO beliefs about what was important for the success of the organization and the cause and effect relationship between these factors. Therefore also skills which the CEO utilizes to shape the organization and organizational knowledge add to the task knowledge that is required to perform or can improve the performance of his or her job specific tasks. Organizational and motivational theory researchers knew already that leading an organization which continually transforms itself and its members requires not only beliefs about the strategic development direction, but also skills or personality germane to actually lead.

These often motivation theoretical components of task knowledge originate from psychological theories of personality and values as well as leadership theories. They are compulsory to create a more *fine-grained approach to task knowledge* which examines dimensions beyond those so far used by leader life cycle or upper echelon theory. This thesis agrees with those researchers, who mostly employed organizational learning theory to emphasize how the learning of a CEO affects

---

[120] See Chen/ Hwang/ Raghu (2010), p. 23.
[121] See ibid., pp. 22-23.

organizational performance[122]. E.g. Wulf and Stubner also talk about a dimension of task knowledge which they frame "position-specific skills"[123]. They much refer to especially organization theoretical research, but do not specify these skills as it is provided in this thesis along with figure 9. Instead, and in accordance to the corresponding research stream they understand their position specific skills as a fit between CEO characteristics and firm strategy[124].

Figure 9[125]
From cognitive constructs to observation

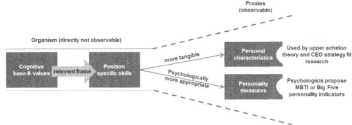

Going further the CEO's personality and values could be directly analyzed via tools from more psychological research, such as the famous Myers-Briggs-Type-Indicator (MBTI)[126] or the Big Five personality indicators[127]. Kauer mentions in his 2008 dissertation on strategic sensemaking that this has been done successfully by some researchers to analyze the world view and personality of CEOs[128].

The MBTI is based on four dichotomies, namely Extraversion (E) – Introversion (I) Sensing (S) – Intuition (N), Thinking (T) – Feeling (F), and Judgment (J) – Perception (P)[129]. Organization psychological research found out so far that generally INTJs are rather visionaries, whereas ESTJs have organizing skills. Likewise some of the most successful contemporary business leaders are claimed to be NTs – intuitive thinkers. The Big Five Model goes beyond as out of it some researchers postulate that people fulfilling the personality dimensions tend to have

[122] See Zhang/ Rajagopalan (2004), p. 484.
[123] See Wulf/ Stubner (2008).
[124] See ibid., p. 7.
[125] Own graphic.
[126] See Kennedy/ Kennedy (2004), p. 38.
[127] See Robbins/ Judge (2009), pp. 107-8.
[128] See Kauer (2008), pp. 62-3.
[129] See Robbins/ Judge (2009), p. 108.

a higher job performance in most occupations. The five dimensions of the model are Extraversion, Agreeableness, Conscientiousness, Emotional Stability and Openness to Experience.

Looking back at the CEO's tasks summarized in Figure 2 in Chapter 1, communicating, controlling, leading, linking, doing and dealing activities fall within his core scope of duties. To put it simple, extraverted people will be better spokespersons, conscientious controllers will be able to keep the overview, some degree of agreeableness and emotional stability can be seen as a precondition to negotiations and linking and finally the strategic doing and dealing tasks might require intuitive thinking or openness to experience. In other words, one should be able to appropriately use one of the above indicators to proxy the psychological components of a person's cognitive base. The more specific application will be done in the next subchapter.

Moreover it shall be mentioned that researchers suggest the use of causal maps as an alternative tool to explore an individuals' idiosyncratic beliefs[130]. They shall give an insight into the belief systems of managers and can be linked to behavior. Nevertheless, they have shown to be highly impractical and more sophisticated[131], hence they shall not be a focus point of this analysis.

Furthermore leadership theories support this view, as even trait theories capture *only* the dimensions that can directly be traced back to personal characteristics or even innate dispositions[132]. Thus behavioral theories enriched the academic discussions by proposing behavioral indicators based on skills such as consideration or initiating structure and others to judge whether a leader is rather employee or production oriented. Finally contingency theories take the situational factors into consideration. They pursue approaches of matching leader styles to situation. These differ only little from the idea of matching personality- or task knowledge-based indicators or characteristics on company performance. E.g. cognitive resource theory points out that a leaders intelligence and experience do affect his reactions under stress and hence his leadership performance. Thus, in a

---

[130] See for this and the following Markozcy/ Goldberg (1995), pp. 305-6.
[131] See Kauer (2008), p. 58, footnote.
[132] See for this and the following Robbins/ Judge (2009), pp. 386-395.

very broad definition even intelligence tests could be used to evaluate the cognitive base of a leader which would be an indicator of some of his skills that constitute task knowledge and hence influence organizational outputs.

Consequently, psychological personality research designates that research on the required knowledge base and skills of a CEO should not only outpace the traditional firm or industry insider-outsider examination. But also fill a concept of task knowledge that contains position-specific skills which are based on the cognitive personality of a leader. Pointing out that research can go beyond the still characteristics based *CEO-Strategy FIT* stream pursued by Wulf and Stubner[133].

The psychological context of task knowledge seems to add another dimension, because the roles which are addressed by the skills rooting in personality like motivating and energizing staff, mobilizing support or networking, belong to those types of task knowledge that can be easily transferred across industry and task contexts[134]. These dimensions form an important, but indirect part of an executive's strategic repertoire and knowledge-base, which leverage their characteristics-based experiences. Therefore, a CEO with such enriched task knowledge will more effectively achieve the missions and steer the organization.

3.3. Framing task knowledge to the context of a CEO

Beginning with knowledge on the organizational and individual level, the psychological components that are deeply interlinked with personality factors have been carved out of a CEO's dispositions and have been linked to task knowledge. Nevertheless, before task knowledge can be put into the context of leader life cycle theory, a *specification of all relevant dimensions of task knowledge* as a construct is necessary within the context of a CEO.

In order to define what accounts for task knowledge in the context of a CEO, researchers looked back to identify the major tasks of this position[135]. It is a common idea that job-related experience will significantly influence a manager's

---

[133] See Wulf/ Stubner (2008), p. 32.
[134] See Thibodeau (2003), p. 48.
[135] See Wulf/ Stubner (2008), p. 6.

strategic observations, interpretations and (re-)actions[136]. Thus a manager's individual knowledge base has to be explored. It is grounded in how deeply and broadly he has collected functional and organizational and personal experiences[137]. One can try to plug the roles and activities which have been derived earlier in this thesis into different domains of knowledge and skills which are required to successfully perform the tasks. As such it embraces a CEO's relevant set of information, skills, procedures and contacts[138].

The activities can generally be either of an internal or external nature. This is reflected in the oldest distinction of performance differences between inside and outside industry and firm hires[139]. This was already noted in upper echelon theory with the focus on industries[140], whereas leader life cycle theory mentions companies. Thus differences in task knowledge between insiders and outsiders are quite obvious and still i.e. research on strategic change differences or skill transferability of outside hires is topical[141].

---

[136] See Kauer (2008), p. 5.
[137] See ibid., p. 3.
[138] See Hambrick/ Fukutomi (1991), p. 725.
[139] See Zhang (2010), p. 335; Hambrick/ Fukutomi (1991), p. 725; Hambrick/ Mason (1984), p. 200.
[140] Nevertheless there is empirical research on insider/outsider differences in the Upper echelon research stream. For this see e.g. Chaganti/ Sambharya (1987), p. 394.
[141] See Zhang/ Rajagopalan (2010), p. 344; Nagel/ Hardin (2011), p. 4.

Figure 10[142]

Deriving skills from the tasks of a CEO's position

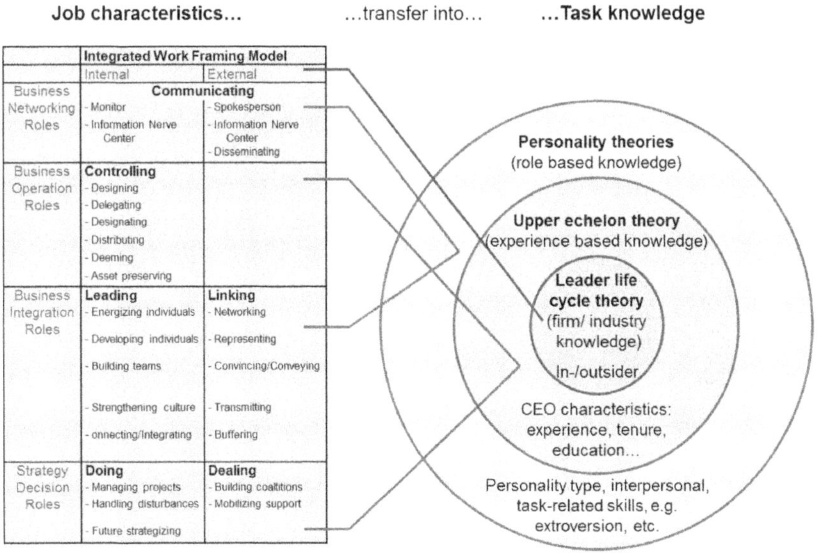

Job characteristics...   ...transfer into...   **...Task knowledge**

	Integrated Work Framing Model	
	Internal	External
Business Networking Roles	**Communicating**	
	- Monitor	- Spokesperson
	- Information Nerve Center	- Information Nerve Center
		- Disseminating
Business Operation Roles	**Controlling**	
	- Designing	
	- Delegating	
	- Designating	
	- Distributing	
	- Deeming	
	- Asset preserving	
Business Integration Roles	**Leading**	**Linking**
	- Energizing individuals	- Networking
	- Developing individuals	- Representing
	- Building teams	- Convincing/Conveying
	- Strengthening culture	- Transmitting
	- onnecting/Integrating	- Buffering
Strategy Decision Roles	**Doing**	**Dealing**
	- Managing projects	- Building coalitions
	- Handling disturbances	- Mobilizing support
	- Future strategizing	

Personality theories (role based knowledge)

Upper echelon theory (experience based knowledge)

Leader life cycle theory (firm/ industry knowledge)

In-/outsider

CEO characteristics: experience, tenure, education...

Personality type, interpersonal, task-related skills, e.g. extroversion, etc.

Predictions about better job performance based on CEO characteristics are often less straight forward. They are based on proxies for job and organizational performance as upper echelon theory suggested. Mostly the operational and strategic roles of a CEO can be covered by his past experiences, which make up his characteristics. Measuring CEO age, functional track, other career experiences, formal education, socioeconomic roots and the financial position allowed for direct predictions on changes in firm performance outcomes[143]. Especially the career experiences and the functional track record directly address the type of work a CEO is already familiar with. Also due to the intuitive frame of upper echelon theory many of those predictors have been widely applied and shown to be mostly valid[144].

Leading, linking and communicating or as Mintzberg named it in an interview "negotiating, venturing, firefighting, and lobbying" are at the core of a CEO's

---

[142] Own graphic.
[143] See Hambrick/ Mason (1984), pp. 198-202.
[144] See Hambrick (2007), p. 335; Yokota/ Mitsuhashi (2008), p. 302; Lawrence (1997).

agenda. Those networking and business integration based roles require role based knowledge and interpersonal skills. Nevertheless they cannot or only partially be captured by upper echelon characteristics. As relying on external characteristics seems to be too convenient, this thesis proposes personality indicators like the MBTI or the big five indicator. This allows to measure for cognitive skills rather than proxiing outside the ""black box" of cognition"[145].

Consequently more task knowledge or experiences and skills specific to the CEO position will enable a CEO to better cope with the strategic postures of the company. To measure the important role top managers play in the strategic decision-making process, this thesis proposes to consider task knowledge as a holistic concept. To analyze the new cognitive capabilities, knowledge, and interests CEOs bring in their activities[146], researchers should concentrate on all the aspects summarized in figure 11.

Figure 11[147]
Integral view on the aspects of task knowledge

The links between job specification and required knowledge have been set in figure 10. Figure 11 frames industry and firm knowledge, experience related knowledge and individual role related knowledge as the relevant parts of the earlier analysis. The knowledge about the latter two can be rather seen as skills than solid and secured knowledge. As a result, CEOs with superior task knowledge should be able to achieve superior organizational outcomes as upper echelon theory suggests.

---

[145] See Markoczy (1997), p. 1228.
[146] See Yokota/ Mitsuhashi (2008), p. 298.

4 The impact of task knowledge on performance over the CEO life cycle

4.1. A theoretical construct of a CEO's task knowledge

Overall, the theoretical foundations of leader life cycle theory and its mechanisms have been described and it could be indicated that it has been empirically validated so far. Further the results of many previous studies indicated that organizational learning theory enriches the leader life cycle theory by a highly relevant theoretical perspective on individual cognitive characteristics[148]. This thesis scrutinized specifically on a psychological construct, task knowledge. It has been carved out of it's interlinks with organizational knowledge as the CEO's position-specific skills. However, as task knowledge has shown to be deeply interlinked with psychology and personality two approaches for measuring it have been introduced. Finally characterizing task knowledge as the skills a leader needs for his roles, three core aspects summarized in figure 10 were falling within this definition to sharpen the predictive power of the construct.

Figure 12[149]

Influence of traditional task knowledge on the shape of the leader life cycle

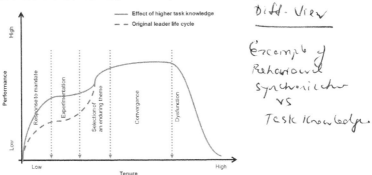

Now the question, how the *holistic or integrated definition of task knowledge* of a CEO fits into leader life cycle theory and how it influences company performance over his tenure in office is addressed. Traditionally Hambrick and Fukutomi placed task knowledge within leader life cycle theory as the information advantage of

---

[147] Own graphic.
[148] See Wulf/ Stubner (2008), p. 32.
[149] Own graphic.

insiders to outsiders, adding that initially with respect to many job activities an insider "is still in unfamiliar waters"[150]. Thus at the time a CEO enters a new position, he possesses the least task knowledge. Correspondingly, the development of task knowledge over the incumbency of a CEO will generally increase. Further researchers identified that he works on this deficit quite fast as his task knowledge learning curve will be steepest early on[151]. The first years are generally those, when a new CEO acquires most of his task knowledge. E.g. Giambatista was able to record the highest performance gains over these years[152]. Later the curve flattens as the CEO becomes more familiar with running his office and only incremental learnings and adaptations in task knowledge occur. In the last stage of a CEO within the life cycle, the task knowledge which became routine and the related absence of learning experiences is seen as a reason for dysfunctioning. Conclusively task knowledge understood as higher industry/firm knowledge and experience will mostly affect the leader life cycle in the initial stages as indicated by figure 12. Consequently, the hypothesizing will focus on the initial years of a CEO's tenure and not specifically consider distinct seasons.

Though, the integrated definition of task knowledge marks a first starting point for a more fine-grained leader life cycle theory as suggested by Hambrick and Fukutomi[153]. Leaders with higher task knowledge with respect to all three dimensions will be more prepared to perform the tasks and activities their job contains. They may hence have a competitive advantage compared to those CEO's with a deficit in especially the experience and skill based aspects of task knowledge. Even though the link to increasing company performance over the tenure may still increase more strongly in the beginning and less intensely later on, some essential skills might make the later performance increase measurably as well. One argument[154] in favor of this hypothesis is that obtaining new knowledge is initially costly and inefficient. In the course of time learning becomes more valuable for the organization as it occurs in the context of greater task knowledge

---

[150] Hambrick/ Fukutomi (1991), p. 725; See for this and the following ibid., p. 725.
[151] See Miller/ Shamsie (2001), p. 728.
[152] See Giambatista (2004), p. 617.
[153] See Hambrick/ Fukutomi (1991), p. 739.
[154] See Miller/ Shamsie (2001), p. 727.

and experience. Thus, even incremental increases might have a substantial impact on company performance. Still, giving further details about concrete seasons would be rather speculative.

Figure 13[155]

Influence of integrated task knowledge on the shape of the leader life cycle

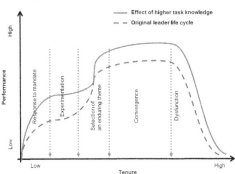

Nevertheless, those leaders who possess higher task knowledge might eventually be still more prone to loneliness due to task disinterest and missing learning curves. Accordingly, the integral task knowledge construct is neither intended to "correct" the general direction, nor to fundamentally change the seasons of how a knowledgeable CEO influences the company performance over time. It rather addresses the links of the neglected variables in the theoretical foundation of the construct. Including experience based characteristics from upper echelon theory as well as personality based skills is the proposed approach in this thesis. The effects of higher experience and role knowledge on the leader life cycle are mapped in figure 13.

Furthermore, the assumptions of the introduced construct of task knowledge within leader life cycle theory have to be clarified. Basically the propositions 3 and 4 of Hambrick and Fukutomi provide a frame also valid for task knowledge[156]. Transferring them directly to task knowledge a first proposition would be:

---

[155] Own graphic.
[156] See Hambrick/ Fukutomi (1991), p. 735.

Proposition A: the longer the incumbency, the stronger will be the association between the leader personality task knowledge and the organizational job characteristics.

Proposition A expresses general tendency of increasing task knowledge over the life cycle. Similarly from a selection perspective new CEO's with higher initial task knowledge can leverage this quality to their advantage. The proposition indicates that task knowledge has to be seen as a variable mediating the relationship between executive tenure and company performance. This forms a precondition, correspondingly true for the other critical trends, to influence the slope of the curve within the curvilinear relationship.

Nevertheless, like the other four factors, task knowledge is limited by moderating variables affecting the manifestations of the seasons. As such, e.g. industry dynamism[157] limits the opportunities for adaptive learning or managerial discretion[158] fosters managers' opportunities to significantly guide the organizational outcome. In an environment of little room for discretion, even a high degree of task knowledge might not satisfactorily support the CEO in realizing an above average performance for his stage of the life cycle. Likewise, e.g. team heterogeneity enables knowledge exchanges or task distribution to those management board members that have the best knowledge[159]. Again, this does not directly measure a CEO's knowledge base.

Proposition B: Task knowledge during the seasons of a CEO's tenure, as well as his or her proposed implications for organizational performance, depend on moderating variables. The more affectionate the moderators, the greater the manifestation of task knowledge during the seasons.

The integrated conceptualization of task knowledge – as outlined here – wants to improve the "incomplete and imprecise, proxies of executives' cognitive frames"[160] yet employed by leader life cycle theory. As it reflects a more fine-grained model, it will improve the predictive accuracy. It offers a theoretically more complete approach to task knowledge by not shying away from the psychological "black box

---

[157] See Henderson/ Miller/ Hambrick (2006), p. 450.
[158] See Hambrick/ Finkelstein (1990), p. 488.
[159] See Carpenter/ Geletkanycz/ Sanders (2004), p. 766; Wong (2008), p. 609.

problem"[161] of cognition. Therefore, hypotheses on the concrete mechanism specifying better task knowledge and how it more effectively and positively influences performance over a CEO's incumbency will be created.

4.2. Hypotheses on the impact of task knowledge on the leader life cycle

As the goal of the thesis is to theoretically analyze the impact of different dimensions of CEO's task knowledge on performance over tenure years, hypotheses on how each aspect of task knowledge will affect performance over the CEO life cycle will be developed.

Initially a clear-cut distinction between differences in the task knowledge of insiders and outsiders has been used to cover task knowledge. However, there are arguments for both, insiders as well as outsiders to be better prepared for a job's tasks based on some contingencies. On the one hand, e.g. if the firm needs strategic change or is challenged by a changing competitive environment outsiders might bring a new strategic perspective into the firm. Their "different approach" of analyzing, framing and working from e.g. an industry which had the same problems before may well equip them for successfully tackling the challenges ahead. They might potentially outperform insiders who are stuck with their paradigm inside the "box" of the company.

On the other hand, outside CEO's might be handicapped compared to insiders[162]. The latter know the environment, the company network, the fruitful and efficient internal communication and information channels or other internal processes and may therefore have an advantage compared to those outsiders[163]. Thus inside CEO's, just due to their deeper understanding of their firms' internal resource, have a solid base to initiate and implement performance increasing strategies[164]. They are however more likely to utilize upon existing organizational capabilities and hence might be more successful in a relatively stable environment.

---

[160] Hambrick (2007), p. 335.
[161] See ibid., p. 335.
[162] See Nagel/ Hardin (2011), p. 9.
[163] See Hambrick/ Mason (1984), p. 200.
[164] See for this and the following Zhang (2010), p. 343.

Zhang or Nagel and Hardin have discovered that for inside CEO's positive effect on firm performance outweigh at low and high levels of strategic change. Agreeing with them, this thesis believes that it is rather the insiders who can gather more relevant task knowledge. Another argument for this choice is, that among many mediating variables Henderson's analysis of industry dynamism revealed that in stable environments the leader life cycle theory predictions as well as the manifestation of the seasons is much clearer[165]. Thus, even though success will still depend on many contingencies, there is a quite reliable amount of literature supporting the value of inside hire skills[166]. Conclusively, if a CEO comes from inside the organization or industry, he will posess a higher task knowledge than an outsider. The elaborated statement is formed as Hypothesis 1.

> *Hypothesis 1: If a CEO initially possesses a higher industry/ firm insider task knowledge, this will positively affect corporate performance during the initial seasons.*

Secondly like in upper echelon theory, individual characteristics have to serve as substitute measures or possible proxies for cognition. The defining question is again which ones are believed to be an appropriate substitute for task knowledge. Besides the upper echelon theory reviewers' general remarks on the reliability of characteristics[167], little research has jet specified demographic characteristics to concretely measure individual knowledge or even task based knowledge. From a knowledge researcher's perspective, Stuart proposes among various third party assessments to measure the average number of years of experience within the profession and the seniority within a company[168]. Framing their position-specific skills, Stubner and Wulf use educational specialization, the educational level, the functional specialization, industry specialization[169]. Thus they partly follow the track of researchers which analyzed the experience base of individual managers

---

[165] See Hambrick/ Mason (1984), p. 200.
[166] See Nagel/ Hardin (2011), p. 10; See Wulf/ Stubner (2008), p. 28; Zhang/ Rajagopalan (2010), p. 335.
[167] See Hambrick (2007), p. 335; Patzelt/ zu Knyphausen-Aufseß/ Nikolw, P. (2008), p. 205.
[168] See Stuart (1999), p. 39.
[169] See Wulf/ Stubner (2008), p. 9.

by measuring (1) their functional experiences and (2) their organizational experiences[170], adding the educational background.

Starting with education, obviously those managers with higher levels of education and an education specialization fitting to their job[171] will potentially indicate higher task knowledge. The reasoning behind this is simply that higher qualifications should prepare for higher level jobs or i.e. specializing in finance before becoming the CEO of a financial services firm should pay off in terms of task knowledge. Different empirical studies confirm this even if the specific education dates back a large number of years. For instance Papadakis and Barwise confirm that CEO education affects strategic decisions[172]. Further Geletkanycz and Black argue that career tracks, dominated by finance, marketing, and general management specifications is positively related to a commitment to the strategic status quo[173].

> Hypothesis 2 (a): If a CEO initially possesses a higher education level based task knowledge, this will positively affect corporate performance during the initial seasons.

> Hypothesis 2 (b): If a CEO initially possesses a higher education specification based task knowledge, this will positively affect corporate performance during the initial seasons.

The executive's career experience can be divided into (a) organizational, (b) functional and (c) industry specialization. All three have been extensively used in other upper echelon contexts. The organizational and a part of the industrial component reflect nothing more than company or industry tenure, which will however be correlated with the CEO tenure depending on insiders or outsiders[174]. It just specifies a bit on how long a CEO is already inside the firm. This might be a bit more precise than the "dummy" 1 or 0 measure. Company tenure was widely used, e.g. by Hambrick in a team heterogeneity context[175] or as CEO tenure by Miller who found that too long tenured CEO's finally resist change and become

---

[170] See Kauer (2008), p. 58;
[171] Education-Job-Industry- or Education-Job-Firm-Fit will have to be measured and decided in the specific cases of a field study. This rather theoretical model will not provide further details. The same is true for the later functional and industry specification variables.
[172] See Papadakis/ Barwise (2002), p. 86.
[173] See Geletkanycz/ Black (2001), p. 17.
[174] See Hambrick/Cho/Chen (1996), p. 672.

"stale in the saddle"[176]. Theoretically longer tenure is often associated with a familiarization with the industry or organization and accordingly a profound knowledge base[177].

Moreover, functional and industry specification can be measured by function subject or type of industry experience. In stable industries matching relevant experiences will proxy for the task knowledge that executives already acquired during their previous jobs. They will be familiar with the patterns of judgment in their industry or function area within their organization[178]. They will develop greater expertise in the disciplines skills and tools in which they specify[179]. The effects of these three factors will be captured by the following hypotheses.

> *Hypothesis 3 (a): If a CEO initially possesses a higher amount of task knowledge as he has stayed longer with the company, this will positively affect corporate performance during the initial seasons.*

> *Hypothesis 3 (b): If a CEO initially possesses a higher amount of task knowledge as he has stayed longer within the industry, this will positively affect corporate performance during the initial seasons.*

> *Hypothesis 3 (c): If a CEO initially possesses a higher functional specification based task knowledge, this will positively affect corporate performance during the initial seasons.*

At this point, the present thesis adds another variable, namely intrapersonal experience heterogeneity. It measures heterogeneity of a manager's functional as well as educational experiences. As the CEO role will demand multidimensional activities and working at many linkages and interfaces with different experts those having experienced different roles before will be better prepared for new challenges. E.g. in dealing with the other board members, such as the CFO, CMO or COO, the CEO will have an advantage in understanding the CFO's objectives and the financial objectives of the firms when he has worked already in such a background. Heterogeneous backgrounds reveal that the manager is used to and

---

[175] See Hambrick/Cho/Chen (1996), p. 672.
[176] Miller (1991), p. 34.
[177] See Kauer (2008), p. 62.
[178] See Hitt/ Tyler (1991), p. 331, 337; See Kauer (2008), p. 59.
[179] See Geletkanycz/ Black (2001), p. 7.

familiar with the networking and linking role of a CEO. Someone who, for instance, worked between his educational degrees might have gathered more of this knowledge. Likewise multiple CEO positions will count as background heterogeneity[180]. Until now this variable was only used in the top management team context as a group variable[181]. Kauer mentions that considering the breadth of functional experience instead of only the depth has never been empirically tested[182]. Nevertheless these "truly generalists"[183] skills of intrapersonal diversity will definitely account for a core part of an executives task specific knowledge.

Hypothesis 4: If a CEO initially possesses task knowledge based on a higher intrapersonal experience heterogeneity this will positively affect corporate performance over all seasons.

The third aspect of task knowledge allows to venture inside the black box of cognition, to examine the psychological processes that account for task knowledge. They are based on task related skills or role related task knowledge in the broader sense. It aims to improve the accuracy of the current task knowledge dimensions by using more appropriate variables – direct psychological personality measures. Either the MBTI or the big five personality indicators can be utilized to measure the task knowledge which is useful for a CEO position as both measures focus on leadership personalities. Applying the MBTI would mean that those leaders falling best into common leader patterns like the those showing NT's will have a better fitting personal task knowledge[184].

The big five personality indicator directly aims to identify those people who will have a higher job performance in most occupations due to a superior personality and knowledge base[185]. The idea is that a higher test result will reveal a higher amount of task knowledge, more accurately than demographic proxies. Using

---

[180] See Nagel/ Hardin (2011), p. 12 argued that multiple CEOs gain a very transferable skill component which shall be measured with this variable.
[181] See Carpenter/ Geletkanycz/ Sanders (2004), p. 765.
[182] See Kauer (2008), p. 62.
[183] Ibid., p. 62.
[184] An interpretation guide like the one of Krebs Hirsh/ Kummerow (1998) could be used for further an individual task-knowledge-fit assessment.
[185] See Robbins/ Judge (2009), p. 109.

causal maps might be a third alternative[186]. Nevertheless the underlying hypothesis should be the following:

Hypothesis 5: If a CEO's personality exhibits initially more role based task knowledge this will positively affect corporate performance over all seasons.

Finally hypothesis 1 – like Hambrick and Fukutomi's original notion of task knowledge – only considers the organizational background and will affect performance as depicted in figure 14(a). Likewise the educational and functional background characteristics will affect rather the initial tenure years, but measure the construct much more appropriately. Further the inclusion of the interfunctional and personality measures might be factors that that indicate superior performance over a longer period within the CEO's tenure. It is based on the belief that CEOs can leverage their interpersonal task related knowledge to a higher degree then their purely functionally or educationally acquired task knowledge. They can potentially benefit from this knowledge and the corresponding competences even when they have chosen their paradigm. In other words, openly and intuitive thinkers performing linking and networking tasks might continue to be more skillful in handling their role related task tactics. Therefore figure 14(b) depicts an alternative estimate of how the integrated measure of task knowledge will affect company performance over the CEO incumbency. Notwithstanding, the integrated approach provides a much more appropriate theoretical measure for a complex cognitive construct such as task knowledge. It will hence increase the predictive accuracy and reflects a more fine grained approach of the impact of a CEO's task knowledge within the leader life cycle.

---

[186] See Tegarden/ Tegarden/ Sheetz (2009), 538.

Figure 14[187]

Predicted effects of CEO tenure on firm performance based on the (a) traditional notion and (b)
integrated notion of task knowledge

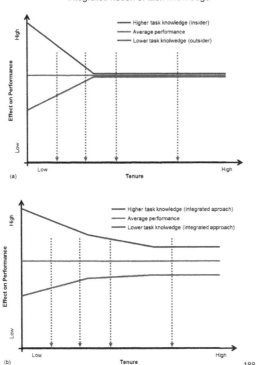

5 Translation of task knowledge into empirically testable variables

5.1. Variable definition

Yet, as Hambrick states previous research already generated quite reliable
predictions by using demographic characteristics. Conclusively the stated
hypotheses on how it does actually affect performance over the tenure need to be

---

[187] Own graphic.
[188] The leader life cycle graphs of how the effect of role related task knowledge are estimated to
infuence performance over the CEO tenure compared to the entire integrated approach can be
viewed in appendix 2.

validated empirically. The concrete empirical test however exceeds the scope of this thesis. Still, ideas on how to theoretically translate the constructs' parts, into measurable variables will be given.

Figure 15 depicts generally how task knowledge can be put into variables. Starting with the insider/ outsider question, a scrutiny into research indicated that finally framing a binary 0/1 dummy variable[189] is frequently used. Of course, an executive who was never employed by the firm is clearly an outsider and someone who is with the firm for a long period is an insider[190]. A borderline case would be someone who is hired and shortly after that quickly promoted to a top executive position. As most of the learning curve, in which task knowledge is advantageous, occurs during the initial 2,5-3 years[191], a solution would be to regard everyone with a less than 3 years of company tenure as an outsider, others as insiders.

Figure 15
Translating task knowledge into empirical variables

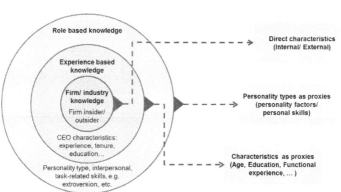

On the experience based variables, the individuals need to be asked for their characteristics. Normally a questionnaire or data base is used for this purpose[192]. After gathering the data they have to be coded according to sensible criteria depending on the sample. Functional specifications could for instance be

---

[189] See Miller/ Shamsie (2001), p. 732
[190] See for this and the following Davidson/ Nemec/ Worrell (2006), p. 42.
[191] See Wulf/ Stubner (2008), p. 17; Gabarro (2007), p.112.
[192] See Carpenter/ Geletkanycz/ Sanders (2004), p. 754-758.

categorized by finance/accounting, legal, productions/operations, administration/ management, marketing/sales, and engineering/R&D[193]. Those can be coded as dummy variables. For the amount of education usually five-point scales from high school to a Ph.D.[194] are utilized[195]. Likewise intrapersonal experience heterogeneity needs to be modeled – presumably also on a scale. Nevertheless, the concrete coding and use of variables will depend on the sample, the breadth of answers given as well as the actual research intentions. Hence a more detailed coding does not provide additional value at this point.

Finally the answers collected from the personality indicators or causal maps can also be broken down into scale point variables and statistically analyzed. For the MBTI this was, however for the purpose of investigating the relationship between students' MBTI scores and their performance in finance exam questions, done by Filbeck and Smith[196]. Alike, e.g. Thoresen et al. statistically coded the big five personality indicator by using random coefficient modeling to test the validity of the Big Five personality traits in predicting overall sales performance in samples of pharmaceutical sales representatives[197]. Finally to give an example, Tegarden et al. explain the steps for analyzing cognitive maps[198].

5.2. Discussion of limitations and implications

Prior research suggests that a CEO's task knowledge as a core variable in the leader life cycle theory can be accurately described by an approximation of inside versus outside hires[199]. To challenge this approach a construct including experience based as well as role related measures was proposed. It undermines the findings of Miller and Shamsie, that learning and experience benefits last a very long time and positively affect performance[200]. The construct offers an

---

[193] See Barker/ Mueller (2002), p. 789.
[194] The scale would consist of "High school, some college, bachelors degree, masters degree, Ph.D".
[195] See Hitt/ Tyler (1991), p. 337.
[196] See Filbeck/ Smith (1996), p. 84.
[197] See Thoresen et al. (2004), p. 835.
[198] See Tegarden/ Tegarden/ Sheetz (2009), p. 544.
[199] See Hambrick/ Fukutomi (1991), p. 725.
[200] See Miller/ Shamsie (2001), p. 738.

explanatory value that surely goes beyond a simple reaffirmation of that which is already understood as Carpenter fears[201]. Still, unlike upper echelon theory, leader life cycle theory requires more empirical tests in concrete business and industry contexts[202].

The task knowledge framework is as such designed for applications within the leader life cycle theory. It may be limited to those applications where an approximation by demographic characteristics is reasonable. Psychologists claim that only direct personality measures can reveal information about the real cognitive bases of a CEO[203]. Independent of this, the proposed approach focuses on the initial seasons during the leader life cycle. Here CEO task knowledge has shown to significantly affect the company performance. As later increases are only incremental, it would be too hypothetical or vague to specify task knowledge's effect in each season. With respect to this, leader life cycle has only shown little support for all five seasons. E.g. Miller and Shamsie confirm only three distinct seasons[204]. As task knowledge permanently increases, no further distinction has been made and should be required.

For an empirical test it seems that data limitations or the time data collection takes from top executives is a very important bottleneck. A further limitation is outlined by the contingencies which are yet unspecified due to a missing empirical test. For instance, industry dependency or at least stability of the environment might limit the influence of task knowledge. Finally the statistical analysis, especially due to high multicollinearities based on the quite different tenure measures needs to be considered in interpreting the results.

From a theoretical point of view, the goal of the proposed framework of task knowledge is to ultimately refine insights on the leader life cycle theory. Hence the profession is urged to empirically test the hypotheses postulated by the thesis at hand. Theoretical implications are that if a successful empirical test follows, a substantial gain in the measurement could be won by accepting only the little

---

[201] See Carpenter/ Geletkanycz/ Sanders (2004), p 770.
[202] See Miller/ Shamsie (2001), p. 739.
[203] See Markoczy (1997), p. 1240.
[204] See Miller/ Shamsie (2001), p. 737.

losses in convenience[205]. As such, this thesis might be a starting point for a continuation of development and refinements in proxying tools for exploring a CEO's cognitive base. Other social or cognitive constructs in upper echelons and leader life cycle theory might refer to the methodologies proposed here. Nonetheless, even if empirics will little differ from those of the original one dimensional construct, this would prove that CEO characteristics or even basic insider/ outsider differentiations can well approximate a CEO's cognitive base. Moreover, it could be an indicator for the power of contingencies, moderating variables and industry specifics in disrupting the task knowledge – organizational outcome relationship. Lastly it would indicate that – besides the in/outsider hard facts – CEO's are more homogeneous with respect to their cognitive bases than previously assumed.

From a practitioners perspective the goal of the proposed framework of task knowledge and the respective empirical test is to ultimately improve the insights on the leader life cycle. It can potentially provide executives with information regarding how they might surmount or overcome the biases associated with their experiences and dispositions[206]. Further they might be able to select their fields of specialization or education to build up the relevant task knowledge for further career steps. Similarly from a human resource or executive search viewpoint a more accurate framework of task knowledge will provide insights on which characteristics or tests reveal the best fitting candidate of a vacant executive position. Further at which stage in the life cycle the CEO is and which learning incentives might be necessary from a principal-agent perspective might be useful[207]. This can help to ensure an advantageous development of task knowledge and thus postpone or prevent task disinterest or staleness. At least it illustrates the importance of learning and task knowledge and their relevance for business decisions and organizational outcomes. Still, although many studies contribute to the link between CEO characteristics, behavior or knowledge and

---

[205] See Markoczy (1997), p. 1240.
[206] See Hambrick (2007), p. 337.
[207] See Erlei/ Leschke/ Sauerland (2007), pp. 202-3.

organizational performance, current designs are unable to evaluate how CEOs can directly improve their effectiveness and efficiency during his activities[208].

6 Conclusion and outlook

The aim of this thesis was to transfer strategy-CEO fit research, organizational learning research as well as leadership-based task knowledge research to the leader life cycle theory. By doing so the thesis at hand followed the call of previous scientists to fill this research gap. It explored the mental and theoretical construct of task knowledge and established hypotheses on the effect of task knowledge of a CEO on company performance throughout the seasons of his tenure.

The original discussion about what a CEO's job including his activities and hence his tasks is, was put up front. It was historically linked to the question of whether leaders matter for organizational performance or not. According to upper echelon theory, they and especially their characteristics, proxying for their experiences, motives, and beliefs are valid indicators for organizational performance – among them, potential task knowledge indicators. Finally the bridge to leader life cycle theory could be built across by contradicting interpretations of CEO tenure's influence on performance. At this point leader life cycle theory and the variables forming its concrete shape were analyzed, among them task knowledge[209].

As a crucial variable within this theory in chapter 3, task knowledge – only defined by in-/outsider distinction – was then put back into a larger context within the knowledge and psychological research. This helped to work out a much more complex and construct of the major psychologically relevant dimensions of task knowledge. Namely personal characteristics based and personality dimensions were added. Further, utilizing the role context of a CEO from chapter 1, the major roles defining a CEO's job could be related to task knowledge, integrating all of its three dimensions. Those are defined as *firm/industry based task knowledge*, *experience based task knowledge* and *role based task knowledge*. The construct was hence named **integrated task knowledge.**

---

[208] See O'Gorman/ Bourke/ Murray (2005), p. 7.
[209] See Hambrick and Fukutomi (1991), p. 723.

Incorporating this construct into leader life cycle theory allows to increase its predictive accuracy and to model a more fine grained approach of the impact of a CEO's task knowledge within the leader life cycle. Concerning this construct, newly *education level, education specification, industry and company tenure, functional specification, intrapersonal experience heterogeneity and role based task knowledge* were used to create hypotheses. For all of them a positive impact of a CEO's task knowledge on the company performance was predicted. Furthermore on the connection between CEO task knowledge and the general slope of the leader life cycle the last two might increase performance continuously over the life cycle in a measurable way.

Chapter five discussed some issues concerning the coding of the influence factors of the concept into variables that can be used in a regression. Further the practical impossibility to depict distinct seasons of the theoretical construct or that a data collection must consider the harsh CEO time constraints form some boundaries. In case of a positive empirical test the theory would stand in line with other recent research endeavors to open the black box of cognition. Though, an empirical rejection would similarly allow for beneficial implications for the research stream. Alike for practitioners, the relevance of task knowledge to business performance is illustrated and could guide the future choice functional or educational specifications or incorporated into search characteristics of head hunters.

Finally, the present thesis successfully sheded light on links between the roles of CEOs, the required task knowledge and further the implications on company performance. While aiming to theoretically analyze the underlying impact over the leader life cycle to close the respective research gaps, its **main contributions** can be summarized as follows:

- Profound derivation of leader life cycle theory out of previous CEO research areas
- Current literature review of the leader life cycle theory and its applications
- Theoretical derivation and conceptualization of task knowledge beyond the scope of previous research
- Application and integration of a more complete approach to task knowledge in the light of the leader life cycle theory

- Derivation of hypotheses and variables awaiting for a further empirical analysis
- Advancement from a pure demographic characteristics based methodology to direct psychological personality measures

Looking ahead, how task knowledge affects strategic decision making or organizational outcomes during the leader life cycle can be incorporated in other, more holistic leader life cycle research programs. Particularly, the effects of task knowledge on moderating variables could create explanatory power. For instance how external moderators like industry dynamism affect task knowledge would further add value[210]. With reference to this, Henderson, Miller and Hambrick examined fast cycled industries like the computer industry. They observed that the organizational outcome was best during the first year of a CEO's incumbency and worsened gradually. This requires a profound explanation from the task knowledge perspective. Such research agendas would shed light on further underlying mechanisms of the task knowledge dimensions as a core factor within the leader life cycle theory.

Besides this, scrutinizing into the mental constructs of task knowledge and adaptive learning might be fruitful for future research. It will be necessary to explain the mechanisms running a human cognitive base – or partially that of a chief executive officer during his tenure. At this point the results and methodology of this thesis can be utilized to generate new research questions at the interface between both disciplines. As an outlook in the psychological disciplines this thesis wants accelerate the impulse towards increasingly opening the black box of cognition and venturing from extremely convenient substitutes to more refined tools for measuring cognitive constructs.

---

[210] See for this and the following Henderson/ Miller/ Hambrick (2006), p. 458.

Table of appendixes

Appendixes

Appendix I: Verbal version of the Critical Trends during a CEO's tenure[211]

Critical trends	1) Response to mandate	2) Experiment-ation	3) Selection of an enduring theme	4) Conver-gence	5) Dys-function
Commitme nt to a paradigm	Moderately strong	Could be strong or weak	Moderately strong	Strong: increasing	Very Strong
Task knowledge	Low but rapidly increasing	Moderate; somewhat increasing	High; slightly increasing	High; slightly increasing	High; slightly increasing
Information diversity	Many soruces: unfiltered	Many sources but increasingly filtered	Fewer sources; moderately filtered	Few sources; highly filtered	Very view sources; highly filtered
Task interest	High	High	Moderately high	Moderately high but diminishing	Moderately low and diminishing
Power	Low: increasing	Moderate: increasing	Moderate: increasing	Strong: increasing	Very strong: increasing

---

[211] Hambrick/ Fukutomi (1991), p. 729.

Appendix II: The impact of the influence of integrating role related task knowledge measures

(a) Influence of higher experience and role related knowledge on the shape of the leader life cycle

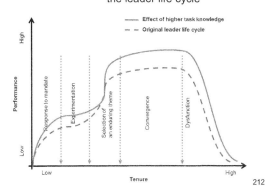

212

(b) Combined influence of integrated task knowledge on the shape of the leader life cycle

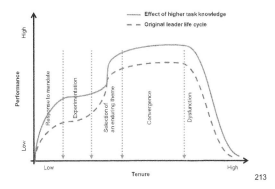

213

---

[212] Own graphic.
[213] Own graphic.

Literature

Anderson, R. C. (1977). The notion of schemata and the educational enterprise: General discussion of the conference. In R. C. Anderson, R. J. Spiro and W. E. Montague (eds.), *Schooling and the acquisition of knowledge* (1984, pp. 415-431). Hillsdale, NJ: Lawrence Erlbaum.

Andone, I. (2009). Measuring the Performance of Corporate Knowledge Management Systems. Informatica Economia, 13(4), 24-31.

Barker, V. L., Mueller, G.C. (2002). CEO Characteristics and Firm R&D Spending. Management Science, 48(6), 782–801.

Beckurts, K.H., Reichwald, R. (1984). Kooperation im Management mit integrierter Bürotechnik – Anwendererfahrungen. München: CW-Publishing.

Bergh, D. D. (2001). Executive retention and acquisition outcomes: A test of opposing views on the influence of organizational tenure. Journal of Management, 27(5), 603–622.

Cannella, A. A. (2001). Upper echelons: Donald Hambrick on executives and strategy. Academy of Managment Executive, 15(3), 36-42.

Carlson S. (1951). Executive Behaviour. Stockholm: Strombergs.

Carpenter, M. A., Geletkanycz, M. A., Sanders, W. G. (2004). Upper Echelons Research Revisited: Antecedents, Elements and Consequences of Top Management Team Composition. Journal of Management, 30(6), 749–778.

Castaldi, R. M. (1986). An Analysis of the Work Roles of CEOs of Small Firms. American Journal of Small Business, Summer 1986, 53-64.

Chaganti, R., Sambharya, R. (1987) Strategic Orientation and Upper Echelon Characteristics. Strategic Management Journal, 8(4), 393-401.

Chen, A., Edgington, T. M. (2005). Assessing Value in Organizational Knowledge Creation: Considerations for Knowledge Workers.MIS Quarterly, 29(2), 279-309.

Chen, A., Hwang, Y., Raghu, T. S. (2010). Knowledge Life Cycle, Knowledge Inventory, and Knowledge Acquisition Strategies. Decision Sciences, 41(1), 21-47.

Dargie, C. (2000). Observing Chief Executives: Analysing Behaviour to Explore Cross-Sectoral Differences. Public Money & Management, 20(3), 39-44.

Davidson, W. N., Nemec, C., Worrell, D. L. (2006). Determinants of CEO Age at Succession. Journal of Management and Governance, 10(1), 35–57.

Davies, J., Thomas, H. (2009). What do business school deans do? Insights from a UK study. Management Decision, 47(9), 1396-1419.

Davis, P. M. (1991). Cognition and learning: A review of the literature with reference to ethnolinguistic minorities. Dallas, TX: Summer Institute of Linguistics.

Drucker, P. (1954). The Practice of Management. New York: Harper & Row.

Drucker, P. (1993). Post-Capitalist Society. New York: Harper business.

Eitzen, D. S., Yetman, N. R. (1972). Managerial change, longevity, and organizational effectiveness. Administratire Science Quarterly, 17, 110-116.

Erlei, M., Leschke, M., Sauerland, D. (2007). Neue Institutionenökonomik. 2nd edn., Stuttgart: Schäffer-Poeschel.

Filbeck, G., Smith, L. L. (1996). Learning styles, teaching strategies, and predictors of success for students in corporate finance. Financial Practice & Education, 6(1), 74-85.

Friedman, J. P. (2007). Dictionary of Business Terms. 4th edn., New York: Barron's Educational Series.

Gabarro, J. J. (2007). When a New Manager Takes Charge. Harvard Business Review, 85(1), 104-117.

Geletkanycz, M. A., Black, S. S. (2001). Bound by the past? Experience-based effects on commitment to the strategic status quo. Journal of Management, 27(1), 3–21.

Giambatista, R. C. (2004). Jumping through hoops: A longitudinal study of leader life cycles in the NBA. The Leadership Quarterly, 15(1), 607-624.

Gourlay, S. (2006). Conceptualizing knowledge creation: a critique of Nonaka's theory. Journal of Management Studies, 43(7), 1415–36.

Haas, M. R., Hansen, M. T. (2002). Are organizational capabilities valuable? An empirical Test of the Pitfalls of leveraging Knowledge. Academy of Management Proceedings, 2002, Business Policy and Strategy Division, 1-6.

Hackman, J.R. (1969). Nature of the Task as a Determiner of Job Behavior. Personnel Psychology, 22(4), 435-444.

Hambrick, D. C., Mason, P. A. (1984). Upper Echelons: The organization as a Reflection of Its Top Managers. Academy of Management Review, 9(2), 193-206.

Hambrick, D. C., Finkelstein, S. (1987). Managerial discretion: A bridge between polar views of organizational outcomes. Research in Organizational Behavior, 9, 369-406.

Hambrick, D. C., Finkelstein, S.(1990). Top-Management-Team Tenure and Organizational Outcomes: The Moderating Roie of Managerial Discretion. Admimstrative Science Quarterly, 35(3), 484-503.

Hambrick, D.C., Fukutomi, G.D.S. (1991). The Seasons of a CEO's Tenure. The Academy of Management Review, 16(4), 719-742.

Hambrick, D. C., Cho, T. S., Chen, M. (1996). The influence of top management team heterogeneity on firms' competitive moves. Administrative Science Quarterly, 41(4), 659-684.

Hambrick, D. C., Finkelstein, S., Mooney, A. (2005). Executive job demands: New insights for explaining strategic decisions and leader behaviors. Academy of Management Review, 30, 472-491.

Hambrick, D. C. (2007). Upper echelons theory: An update. Academy of Management Review, 32(2), 334-343.

Hemphill, J. K. (1960). Dimensions of executive positions. Columbus, OH: Bureau of Business Research, Obio State University.

Henderson, A.D., Miller, D., Hambrick, D.C. (2006). How Quickly Do CEOs Become Obsolete? Industry Dynamism, CEO Tenure, and Company Performance, Strategic Management Journal, 27(5), 447-460.

Hitt, M. A., Tyler, B. B. (1991). Strategic Decision Models: Integrating Different Perspectives. Strategic Management Journal, 12(5), 327-351.

Jaw, Y.-L., Linb, W.-T. (2009). Corporate elite characteristics and firm's internationalization: CEO-level and TMT-level roles. The International Journal of Human Resource Management, 20(1), 220–233.

Kauer, D. (2008). The Effect of Managerial Experiences on Strategic Sensemaking. Wiesbaden: Deutscher Universitäts-Verlag.

Kennedy, R. B., Kennedy, D.A. (2004). Using the myers-briggs type indicator in career counseling. Journal of Employment Counseling, 41(1), 38-44.

Kesner, I., Sebora, T. (1994). Executive Succession: Past, Present & Future. Journal of Management, 20(2), 327-372.

King, A. W., Zeithaml, C. P. (2003). Measuring Organizational Knowledge: A Conceptual and Methodological Framework. Strategic Management Journal, 24(8), 763-772.

Kotter, J. P. (1990). A force for change how leadership differs from management. New York: Free Press.

Krebs Hirsh, S., Kummerow, J.M. (1998). Introduction to Type in Organizations. 3rd edn., Mountain View (CF): CPP Inc.

Lakshman, C. (2005). Top Executive Knowledge Leadership: Managing Knowledge to Lead Change at General Electric. Journal of Change Management, 5(4), 429-446.

Lawrence, B. S. (1997). The black box of organizational demography. Organization Science, 8(1), 1-22.

Mackey, A. (2008). The effect of CEOs on firm performance. Strategic Management Journal, 29(12), 1357-1367.

Matthaei, E. (2010). The Nature of Executive Work: A Case Study. Wiesbaden: Gabler.

Manner, M. H. (2010). The Impact of CEO Characteristics on Corporate Social Performance. Journal of Business Ethics, 93(1), 53-72.

Markoczy, L. (1997). Measuring Beliefs: Accept No Substitutes. Academy of Management Journal, 40(5), 1228-1242.

Markóczy, L., Goldberg, J. (1995). A Method for Eliciting and Comparing Causal Maps. Journal of Management, 21(2), 305-333.

McCarthy, D. (2000). View from the top: Henry Mintzberg on strategy and management. Academy ot Management Executive, 14(3), 31-39.

Merriam-Webster Dictionary (2011a). Repertoire. http://www.merriam-webster.com/dictionary/repertoire, 19.06.2011.

Merriam-Webster Dictionary (2011b). Knowledge. http://www.merriam-webster.com/dictionary/knowledge, 19.06.2011.

Michl, T., Welpe, I., Spörrlel, M., Picot, A. (2010). Der Einfluss affektiver Zustände auf den strategischen Entscheidungsfindungsprozess. G. Schreyägg & P. Conrad (eds.), *Managementforschung* (20, pp. 79-112), Wiesbaden: Gabler.

Mintzberg, H. (1973). The Nature of Managerial Work. New. York: Harper & Row.

Mintzberg, H. (1989). Mintzberg on Management: Inside our strange world of organizations. New York: The Free Press.

Mintzberg, H. (1994). Rounding Out the Manager's Job. Harvard Business Review 36(1), 11–25.

Mintzberg, H. (2009). Managing. San Francisco: Berrett Koehler Publishers Inc.

Miller, D. (1991). Stale in the saddle: CEO tenure and the match between organization and environment. Management Science, 37(1), 34–52.

Miller, D., Shamsie, J. (2001). Learning across the life cycle: Experimentation and Performance among the Hollywood Studio Heads, Strategic Management Journal, 22(8), 725-745.

Nagel, G., Hardin III, W.G. (2011): The Transferability of CEO Skills, Draft, Financial Management Association Online, http://www.fma.org/Prague/ Papers/The_Transferability_of_CEO_Skills.pdf, 04.07.2011, 1-43.

Nishii, L., Gotte, A., Raver, J. (2007). Upper Echelon Theory Revisited: The Relationship Between Upper Echelon Diversity, the Adoption of Diversity Practices, and Organizational Performance. CAHRS Working Paper Series, Paper 461, 1-14.

Nonaka, I., Takeuchi, H. (1995) The Knowledge-Creating Company: How Japanese Companies Create the Dynamics of Innovation. New York/ Oxford: Oxford University Press.

O'Gorman, C., Bourke, S., Murray, J. A. (2005). The Nature of Managerial Work in Small Growth-Orientated Businesses. Small Business Economics, 25(1), 1-16.

Papadakis, V. M., Barwise, P.(2002). How Much do CEOs and Top Managers Matter in Strategic Decision-Making? British Journal of Management, 13(1), 83–95.

Patzelt, H., zu Knyphausen-Aufseß, D., Nikolw, P. (2008).Top Management Teams, Business Models, and Performance of Biotechnology Ventures: An Upper Echelon Perspective. British Journal of Management, 19(3), 205–221.

Reutzel, C. R., Belsito, C. A. (2010). Examining the relative influence of upper echelons ties on IPO underpricing. International Entrepeneurial Management Journal, http://dx.doi.org/10.1007/ s11365-010-0163-y, 1-14.

Robbins, S., Judge, T. (2009). Organizational Behavior. 13th edn., Upper Saddle River: Pearson Prentice Hall.

Seaton, J. L. Boyd, M. (2010). Theo organizational Leadership of the post Baby Boom Generation: An Upper Echelon Theory Approach. Academy of Entrepreneurship Journal, 13(2), 69-77.

Stuart, T.A. (1999). Intellectual Capital: The new wealth of organizations. New York: Doubleday.

Tegarden, D., Tegarden, L, Sheetz, S. (2009). Cognitive Factions in a Top Management Team: Surfacing and Analyzing Cognitive Diversity using Causal Maps. Group Decision & Negotiation, 18(6), 537-566.

Thibodeau, J. (2003). The Development and Transferability of Task Knowledge. Auditing: A Journal of Practice & Theory, 22(1), 47-67.

Thoresen, C. J., Bradley, J. C., Bliese, P. D., Thoresen, J. D. (2004). The Big Five Personality Traits and Individual Job Performance Growth Trajectories in Maintenance and Transitional Job Stages. Journal of Applied Psychology, 89(5), 835-853.

von Krogh, G., Nonaka, I., Rechsteiner, L. (2011). Leadership in Organizational Knowledge Creation: A Review and Framework. Journal of Management Studies, doi: 10.1111/j.1467-6486.2010.00978.x, 1-38.

Wong, S. (2008). Task knowledge overlap and knowledge variety: the role of advice network structures and impact on group effectiveness. Journal of Organizational Behavior, 29(1), 591-614.

Wu, S., Levitas, E. Priem, R. L. (2005). Ceo Tenure and Company invention under differing levels of technological dynamism. Academy of Management Journal, 48(5), 859–873.

Wulf, T., Miksche, J., Roleder, K., Stubner, S. (2010). Performance over the CEO Lifecycle –A Differentiated Analysis of Short and Long Tenured CEOs. HHL Working Paper, 88, 1-37.

Wulf, T., Stubner, S. (2008). Executive succession and firm performance – the role of position-specific skills. HHL Working Paper, 86, 1-33.

Yokota, R., Mitsuhashi, H. (2008). Attributive change in top management teams as a driver of strategic change. Asia Pacific Journal of Management, 25(2), 297–315.

Zhang, Y., Rajagopalan, N. (2004). When the known devil is better than an unknown God: An empirical study of the antecedents and consequences of relay CEO successions. Academy of Management Journal, 47(4), 483-500.

Zhang, Y., Rajagopalan, N. (2010). Once An Outsider, Always An Outsider? CEO Origin, Strategic Change, And Firm Performance. Strategic Management Journal, 31(3), 334–346.

Document Nr. V196180
http://www.grin.com
ISBN 978-3-656-22420-4